THE SHAPE OF A YEAR

THE SHAPE OF A YEAR

Jean Hersey

Illustrated by John Pimlott

CHARLES SCRIBNER'S SONS New York

A-2.66[V]

Printed in the United States of America
Library of Congress Catalog Card Number 67-13158

For Connie

who helps to shape each year

Acknowledgments

Appreciation is expressed to the editors of Woman's Day (a Fawcett publication) and American Home for permission to use material which has appeared in their publications. Also I wish to thank Adelle Davis for permission to use recipes from *Let's Cook It Right* published by Harcourt Brace and World; Renee Taylor for a recipe from *Hunza Health Secrets* published by Prentice Hall; Witter Bynner for a few lines from *The Way of Life: According to Laotse* published by The John Day Company; Lilja Rogers for her poem which appeared in the Saturday Evening Post.

I am grateful to family, friends, and neighbors, who, as mentioned here, have been so important in setting the shape of our year. Also I would particularly like to thank Ann Bridgman and June Schlegel for their careful typing of the manuscript.

Contents

If your true nature has the
creative force of Nature itself,
wherever you go you will see
all things as fishes leaping
and wild geese flying

ZEN PHILOSOPHY

Year's beginning

QUIET AND SMOOTH, fresh and untouched the new snow lies across our meadow. Its pristine surface catches the sunlight, and tree shadows stretch like great blue pencils over the unbroken white. The snow folds gently over rocks and hummocks half concealing, half revealing a variety of different shapes.

So lies our year ahead, its basic ingredients sun and shadow and suggested shapes of things to come. I wonder what we will do with this year, what it will do with us, and what together we and life will create during the twelve months ahead.

Our house stands in the midst of these rolling snowfields, Soon my husband will shovel narrow paths to the terrace bird feeders, to the woodpile north of the house, to his shop. Joe comes to plow our road and drive. With his bright red tractor he pushes great three and four foot drifts up against the split rail fence that borders the vegetable garden. Birds, deer, squirrels, rabbits, foxes, all leave their footprints. A little kitten-soft but ferocious shrew always wiggles a trail just under the snow's surface near the roses and perennials. Neighbor dogs romp in the snow and our grandsons Jesse and Jeff ski criss-cross patterns over the rolling slopes. This pure white meadow of snow graciously receives the imprint of the life that comes to it. The man-made patterns merge and mingle with the moving tree shadows, the sun, and the blowing flakes.

A new year is a gift, a small piece of infinity, to do with as we will. Things happen. We grow (we hope), and we learn willy nilly. Life moves around us, life moves through us to others, and the year gradually accepts its pattern. We give, we take, we resist, we flow. Our reachings, acceptances, rejections, our hesitancies, courage, fears, and our loves, all these form the shape of the year for each of us, as individuals, as part of a family, as a member of a community.

No two years are ever alike, no two Januarys. Every snowflake differs from the next one, no daffodil in the meadow is absolutely identical with its neighboring daffodil, and no two birds sing the same song.

Each year we think about different things, have different projects, goals, and challenges. There was the year we built the brick terrace, the summer of the trip to Switzerland and the arrival of a new grandson. There was the camping holiday to California with that unforgettable week living five feet from a madly rushing stream on a Colorado mountainside. There was the spring my last new book came out, the Listening Courses Bob and I led together at Wainwright House. All these things have marked, molded, and made every year rich and challenging in its own way.

The valley where we live remains, of course, basically unchanged. Pop's Mountain stands guard to the west with its fringe of evergreens at the top looking down on the overgrown wood road where long years ago the British marched up to Danbury. The melodious and ever active stream flows through the valley and along our meadow to merge with the Saugatuck River beyond. The summer suns grow our garden each season, and a harvest moon shines down. Winds blow icy cold in winter, soft and caressingly warm in spring and summer. Stars prick through a black night the year round. They delight us with their brilliance and always arouse the question —what and who can be way off there in space?

As we commence this new January we start with many changes in our personal lives. My husband is no longer a New York City commuter. He drives daily to an interesting new kind of work three-quarters of an hour away in Rye. All of a sudden we have a wonderful thing called An Evening. This we never had when he shared his days with the New Haven Railroad. While, unhappily, some of our erstwhile neighbors have moved from the valley, still we are surrounded by new friends. Down the road on the bridge over the Saugatuck the sign BEWARE OF TROLLS on the fence rail has been painted over and now it says RIVER STYX. Neighbor children have grown up and into high school.

New books added to our shelves have led us along different paths of pleasure and learning. The garden is a little different each season. Bob is in the midst of painting the outside of the house a lovely rich brown with interesting green-gold doors. And this winter my hooked rug is a white unicorn.

Abby Glover no longer comes to clean and iron. She first came into our lives some years ago and I have always thought it was because we had a greenhouse and a cat! She lives just up the road in the glen with her son and seventeen cats and chickens, and is now in her eighties. Occasionally she walks over to see me. I often go to visit with her and buy her rare, huge, and heavenly eggs. She still shares tales of the past, local lore and old country ways with me. Now and then I take her for a drive, and this is a mutual pleasure.

When I sit in Mrs. Glover's kitchen with a few kittens in my lap she tells me stories about the old days before the town of Valley Forge was flooded to make the reservoir above the glen. She speaks freely of the time when He (her husband) used to burn charcoal in the woods just above our house and deliver it by horse and a great high-sided wagon to the brass foundries in Bridgeport fifteen miles off. She also tells me about how He (her son, now fiftyish) first learned to walk and where He took his first step. Sometimes in listening I get her "He's" mixed.

As we visit together, Mrs. Glover usually draws her rocker close by the gleaming old-fashioned wood stove as if she cannot get enough warmth. I miss her regular presence in the house, but we now have Elsie from Kentucky who is large and black and always smiling, except when she is laughing or singing hymns. Elsie invariably calls me "darling" and her great warmth fills the house every Thursday while she sings her way from one end to the other, leaving a trail of spotless rooms behind her.

As the new year approaches, we review the pattern of the old one. What shall we keep and what shall we toss out? There is much to hold on to and also many changes to make. Our underlying theme for this year is to be quality not quantity. In the months ahead we will do more of less, rather than more and more. In other words, engage ourselves more deeply in fewer activities, and become involved more thoroughly in each single one. We plan to read fewer books but read those more lingeringly. In our garden we'll plant fewer things and take better care. The events in our days will be fewer and we shall appreciate each one more.

❀ 5

Life tends to be full of multitudinous contacts with people while true relationships are more rare. This is our year to limit mere contacts and explore relationships more deeply.

On New Year's Day an exciting new door opens. We look ahead—wondering, waiting, and ready.

PART I

Season of indoor living—of waiting—of expectancy

THESE ARE THE MONTHS when our lives are lived largely within four walls, under a man-made roof, and snugly protected against wind and weather. Intermittent forays into the world of nature are brief, and when we venture forth we are bundled in heavy clothing against the elements. How we welcome our warm homes again!

Short days are followed by long evenings of glowing fires, of books, and pleasant conversations into the night. On the wildest of stormy days we find ourselves dreaming of next summer's vacations or perhaps planning special garden features and delving into the provocative seed catalogues. This is a time for dreaming. All through these weeks there is an undercurrent of anticipation, a waiting, an expectancy, a preparation.

Nature also has drawn within herself. The vitality of all that grows is no longer visible in leaf and flower, but lies hidden deep in the heart of seed and root. Nature rests and restores herself, gathers her forces for the furious activity of spring and summer.

This is a creative hesitation like the pause in music between the notes that accents the tones and helps form the underlying melody—the basic shape of our year.

I

January begins a new year, crisp and fresh and white

JANUARY MORNINGS AT SEVEN are like opals, soft, milky white and pink around the edges. The January sun rises silvery white, bright but not warm, and a mist like an aura hovers over the south meadow.

One morning early as we ate breakfast, Bob was eyeing a cluster of many colored Christmas tree balls lying in one of the upholstered chairs. We had dismantled the tree the day before.

"They look," said he sipping his coffee, "as if they were waiting for a goose to come along and hatch them."

"It would have to be a golden goose," I replied watching the stars laid on their shiny surfaces by the early sun streaming in the windows. Obviously no ordinary goose could sit on these bits of Christmas magic.

Those many colored balls were the spark needed to set off my annual house cleaning. I'd begin by putting away Christmas. First the crèche figures. A couple of weeks ago Mary and Joseph and the Babe in the manger composed a scene of pure wonder in the corner of the living room. But now in January I noticed that they were a little chipped, and in places their paint was wearing off.

I sat down in the middle of the floor in the sun to slip the rainbow-colored balls back in their boxes. Each one reflected an image of myself, and a piece of the room. Sometimes even more shone in the glossy surface—other Christmases, other years.

I saw again the first Christmas Bob and I were married. Our tiny tree had just three balls, for we had been married exactly three weeks. Then came subsequent Christmases with a huge tree, and first one, then two, then three stockings hung by the fireplace. Bob was filling those, I was pressing the Santa Claus suit, while our three children Joan, Bob, and Tim slept upstairs. These brief glimpses flashing pleasantly by were soon laid away with the balls in tissue. Today was today and there was house cleaning ahead.

How can you house clean in the spring when all outdoors issues an irresistible invitation? I can't, so I do it now.

In winter we have no love affair with Nature, just a passing friendship, respect, appreciation. We each go our separate, unrelated ways with a good stout wall between us. And now my way takes me into cupboards, closets and drawers, curious to see what is there and eager to eliminate the surplus. House cleaning is fascinating, frustrating, and necessary. It not only gains you clean cupboards, but it's a sort of combined treasure hunt and a trip into the past, and I like trips to anywhere.

A good time to begin our new philosophy of quality not

quantity, I thought, gathering up old catalogs, magazines, and lamps broken beyond repair, I am tempted to eat up the old bottles of pills that I find in the medicine cabinets, especially if they are expensive prescriptions, for it's then that the Scotch in me comes out. I can seldom remember what they are for, but surely they will contribute something of value. Bob takes a dim view of this and firmly says, "Throw them out."

What about the books we are going to read some day but haven't in the past ten years we've had them? Though Bob's heart is in the right place it is fatal to ask his help in sorting books. He begins to read them all, then I do, and two hours later we have just as many books.

In the backs of closets along with an ancient wicker tray and a spare set of vacuum cleaner attachments, I find faded curtains, a rusty flashlight with no batteries, and a number of other things no longer in use but still too good to throw out! This is the frustrating part.

"I'm going to pretend," I said firmly to Bob at dinner that night, "that we are moving to Switzerland." (A country we happen to love.) "We are traveling by air and all excess baggage is a dollar a pound."

Obviously we can't take the spare vacuum cleaner attachments. This point of view helps eliminate a three-foot-high pile of Orchid Bulletins, some torn pillow covers, seed packages years old, outdated automobile maps, and six framed pictures of people we never knew, along with two cracked bowls and X-rays of bones long since mended. Whenever I reach the bottom of a drawer there always remains one paper clip, one elastic band, one box of paper matches with two left, a screw, a mysterious key, a thumbtack, a hairpin, an eraser, and a bottle of dried ink. These I firmly turn into the scrapbasket—sometimes even if the elastic is still bouncy.

What fuzzy edges grow on our thinking when we live with a background of clutter. I make another rule—"have I used this or worn it in the last year—or has it contributed beauty?" Circulation, we are told, is a law of being. So give the object away, let it go back into circulation.

As piles move out of our cupboards and closets, I can practically feel my growing edge sharpen. A cool, airy feeling develops in my head, and it isn't all a recent haircut. What a joy to contemplate a cleared-off desk, a neat pile of sheets and towels, and bookshelves arranged so that when we buy a new volume we don't have to throw away an old one.

House cleaning also has its touching moments—old pictures of family and friends can be particularly moving. You see people as they were many years ago and you know them as they are today. There is always some quality in the old picture that hints at what is to come, at what you find now. Sometimes a promise in the old photo is not fulfilled today. This can be a little sad.

One morning while deep in the linen closet I came upon my mother's tablecloth, embroidered and snowy white, which she gave us when we were married. We use it for family events of great importance. As I ran my hand over the smooth, fresh surface, a whole series of festivities came alive again—our daughter's wedding, the party when Bob Jr. returned from Korea, and a few years later another when he brought his bride. There was the gay evening for our younger son Tim's engagement party, and the housewarming for everyone when we first moved here to Connecticut.

But what do you do with a solid silver soap dish? We use soap dishes on camping trips. But I can't quite envision a silver one at the brink of a stream in the Rockies while I wash Bob's socks. But because it was my mother's I put it back into the linen closet. Resolutions are made to be bent once in a while.

On a high remote shelf I came across two packages of wild rice. We bought them while camping in Cass Lake, Minnesota. I put them away for a special occasion since they were so choice. And now, two years later, here they were next to some hard as a-rock marshmallows. The wild rice was simply vibrating with life—and not the edible kind! "Let that be a lesson to you," said I to myself. "No more hoarding for a rainy day or special occasion—but use something new and exciting right away."

Bob with a resigned and painful sigh sorts things in his drawers, closet and desk. House cleaning, I suspect, is essentially a female pursuit. However, he yields to coaxing and I eventually gathered a pile to be thrown out from his room. Suddenly one morning, I'd had enough. The sun was streaming down outside and here was I deep in a cupboard of Kodachromes all falling out of their boxes and some plastic table mats we never use. Never, never will I buy another THING, I tell myself adamantly. This is good for the budget because for weeks afterwards I can pass through any gift shop, even the Pottery Corner, usually my undoing, and resist everything.

Plastic table mats went but I couldn't face those Kodachromes. So I went down the road to play the recorder with Trudy. Is it a feminine vagary to tend to bog down in the midst of a project or just a personal one of mine? Trudy lives by the "River Styx" where the bridge crosses over the Saugatuck and we often play duets together, she on the soprano recorder and I on the tenor. This particular day we played Elizabethan tunes and Shakespearean melodies, along with Bach and Mozart, and some Russian music. Since Bob plays the soprano recorder we have a lot of duet books. I also took a package of home-grown, homemade frozen grape juice for refreshments.

Next morning I was all ready for the final house cleaning. But I'll have to confess I began on the far side of the Kodachromes. It would take a three-day blizzard to do them properly. I turned on Beethoven's Pastoral Symphony good and loud and plunged into the few remaining kitchen cupboards. Soon the whole house was a poem of neatness and order and the linen closet fragrant with a spray of lavender. Two weeks before whenever I had opened the linen closet door something had fallen out on me!

I was contentedly telling myself what a strong character I had been to throw away so much. Then I remembered one last desk drawer. Tucked in the back of it was a wooden stick. About three years ago when our grandson Jeff, aged ten, had come for a visit, he had spent a rainy afternoon working in Bob's shop.

"Grandma, I have a present for you," he called as he came in the door.

"Yes, darling, what is it?" I said, moving myself out of the strawberry shortcake dough I was kneading.

In his hand lay a most mysterious object, a round, inch-thick dowel stick about eight inches long. Seven little holes in a row were bored one inch apart down one side. A small whittled stick fitted in the top hole.

"Why Jeff dear, how lovely, and how thoughtful of you," I said. "What is it?"

"Well, you see, Grandma, it is a calendar. One hole is for each day. Sunday is the hole at the top. You have to know this. Monday is the next one down, and Tuesday the next. You have to know this, too. Then you go all the way down to Saturday. You put the little peg in the top hole on Sunday morning and every night before you go to bed move it down a hole. Then you always know what day it is. Wherever the peg is, that's the day. You see, Grandma?"

I saw. I also saw again how he had stood there looking as I am sure Thomas Edison looked when he made the first light bulb and it lit. I'll never forget the excitement in Jeff's eyes as he handed me the stick to examine, nor his delight when he hung it up and showed it to his grandfather that night. Ceremoniously we set the peg in the proper hole for the next day before we went to bed.

For several years the little "calendar" occupied a prominent position. It had been taken down, I suppose, for cleaning of summer tenants and now it lay unused in my drawer. Was it useful—was it beautiful? I tucked it affectionately back in the far corner of the drawer.

To live properly you must have roots. Roots take different forms and shapes.

Now that the house is all neat and in order, perhaps this is the time to take a tour. Entering the front door you face a glass wall leading into our small 10 x 12 greenhouse. The greenhouse juts into the house itself. This means that we live in a flourishing garden the year round. It's rather nice to be this intimate with a small tropic. It is a tropic, too, because it is filled mostly with orchids.

Step in, with the greenhouse on your left, and you are in the dining area. Double glass doors open wide so we eat with the orchids just a few feet away and at the same time smell that good scent of warm earth and growing plants—and, of course, the deep fragrance of the orchids themselves. People are always surprised to learn how many varieties are sweet scented.

Directly opposite the doors of the greenhouse is the kitchen. When I cook I look across at the flowers. Pass beyond dining area, kitchen, and greenhouse and you are in the living room. Facing you across the room is the fireplace, bookshelves, and our favorite picture. This picture over the mantel seems three dimensional and suggests birds flying on and on and away into the distance.

The living room has two great windows—one to the north and one to the south. When we are not living in the greenhouse we are living in the meadow, for the field is close beyond the pane of glass. We have outside lights that shine over the terrace into the meadow. While snug by the fire we can watch a blizzard of snowflakes blowing in marvelous swirls.

In the middle of the living room ceiling at the moment hangs a fabulous and immense kite sent to us for Christmas by Bob Jr. and Susan in California. It is two or three different shades of fuchsia, scarlet and orange. The color scheme suggests something Oriental, or maybe Persian. It requires 500 feet of nylon string which tests to 50 pounds! We can hardly wait for kite weather to fly it.

The house itself is eighty feet long and lies east and west. Today sunlight streams in all the windows. The overhang is cleverly arranged so that in summer no sun comes. Walk on through the living room and you pass more bookcases and a north window where African violets grow. Now you are in the bedroom end of the house. Beyond this is the sleeping porch where we sleep in summer. From here we listen to the sound of the brook, smell wisteria in May, spice pinks in June, and meadow grass the whole growing season. Outside, along the south side of the house, is the brick terrace designed by our architect son Bob. A few years ago we built this ourselves, following his blueprint. To the north of the house is a large and handsome woodpile for which Bob Sr. is responsible. Outside the kitchen, flanked by lilac bushes, stands a little separate building connected by the grape arbor. This is Bob's shop where he happily repairs, fixes, and builds. Beyond that and bordering the drive as you come in is the vegetable garden where we raise all our summer produce and freeze plenty besides. Our six acres, filled with wild flowers, are surrounded and crossed by ancient stone walls.

On the brick terrace we have two small 6 x 12 flower beds, one for roses and one for perennials. These are our only areas of cultivated flowers. Both these beds are near enough to the house so we in summer catch the fragrance of the blossoms in every room. As I sit at my desk, a mere few feet beyond the window a ruby-throated humming bird sips nectar at a delphinium bloom.

"Perhaps we should go deer hunting tomorrow," said Bob. Before turning out lights for the night he had just stepped outside the front door to look at the stars that were large and close and brilliant. It was Friday. "The weather should be fine with all those stars, and the snow is about right," he added.

It wasn't too deep for woods walking.

"Great idea," I replied, "and let's get Janet."

Janet, one of our neighbors down the road, is a beautiful blend of the practical and the slightly fey. Her many enthusiasms include walking in woods. Since we've known her we have mutually explored quite a lot of wilderness in Weston together.

Janet said she would be up for breakfast at eight. Well fortified with griddle cakes and sausage, we put on boots, woolly scarves and mittens.

Our kind of deer hunting doesn't involve guns or venison, but binoculars and a kind of alertness, nothing more. We follow trails through the Water Company land looking for a deer, or two, or a half dozen. Adjoining our place to the north stretches unbroken wilderness all the way to Redding. Woodland, meadows, old wood roads and brooks, all belonging to the Bridgeport Hydraulic Company, border a reservoir. In this enchanted forest we spend many week-end hours walking, especially during the winter months.

A herd of white-tailed deer live in this region, fifty or more. If you follow their trails, tread carefully and quietly, you usually come upon some. Last fall one of the neighbors up on Wells Hill woke in the night. He thought he was dreaming when outside the window in the light of a full moon he saw the whole herd grazing in his field. In a frenzy of excitement he woke the family, and telephoned his immediate neighbors. These calls were received with mingled feelings—it was three a.m. We've never seen the whole herd, but we often discover five or six when we go deer hunting.

By nine, Janet and Bob and I were off. We went up through Indian Meadow and beyond a grove of pines. Under the lower branches we saw places where deer had bedded for the night and packed down the needles. The winter woods that morning were green and white. Green hemlocks trailed their lower branches with tips caught and held by the snow. Now and again a startled grouse with a great flourish of wings indignantly flew off. Quantities of tracks led everywhere—rabbit, fox (whose prints resemble those of a small dog). There were some tracks too large for a mouse, too small for a raccoon, with a trail dragged through the middle. An opossum perhaps? And, of course, deer tracks were everywhere. We chose one set in the snow which was well packed and following them was easy.

We must have walked an hour or so through lovely, quiet snowy woods when we stopped at the sight of a doe and two fawns about two hundred feet ahead. The watchful mother saw us first and gracefully bounded over the curve of the hill followed by the appealing, spotted twin fawns. Her white tail flipped up with each leap, it was a beautiful sight. Nothing is more graceful than the way a deer moves over the ground. She seemed not quite on it and scarcely off it. Each motion was pure rhythm.

The sun that had been growing hazier and hazier disappeared and tiny snowflakes fell, making a delicate sifting sound on ground and trees. When we stopped there was only the sound of the snow falling. This change in weather brought a hush to the forest. The black water of a slow-moving, ice-rimmed stream received the new snow in silence.

There was a brush of white spreading over the undergrowth and the pine and hemlock branches. Snow was catching on the laurel, the rough bark of the hickory trees, and outlining the limbs of oaks and pines all the way to the top. Each golden-brown beech leaf was growing a white fur ruff. We paused to look at a sapling evergreen mysteriously sawed off about six feet above the ground. It was then we saw another deer, a large buck and not fifty feet away. Because we had been standing still he had not noticed us as he came up over a little rise. We all had a good look with the binoculars. You could even see his eyelashes. The eyes of a deer are wonderfully soft, liquid and brown. Their coats are smooth and this one was dusted white. In a few moments he saw us and streaked off taking each stone wall with a fine leap. The white-tailed deer are capable of a thirty-foot horizontal leap!

We had just turned back when we saw our fifth deer, far off and indistinct because of the snow in the air.

At home tufts of snow were caught against the house wall. Birds were burrowing through the inch or two on the feeders kicking it aside to get at their seed. We brushed it away for them, refilled the suet stick and scattered more food.

Bob built a large fire in the fireplace. Janet took off her shoes and stockings and toasted her bare feet. I heated up soup I'd been making for about a week with bones and all sorts of leftovers and our own parsley from the freezer. It was thick and hot and delicious. As we drank soup, we watched the birds. A single cardinal against the snow is a sight to cheer you. Something to store up in your mind to recall in a lonesome moment.

This is the month when Weather comes in capital letters, and can be seen, heard and felt, and in no uncertain terms. I'm not tempted by postals of sunny beaches and great tropical blossoms that arrive from friends in Florida, Nassau, and the Virgin Islands. I happen to like January in Connecticut.

One day the snow falls quietly, gently, purposefully from a leaden sky, with white drifts folding softly into sculptured shapes around the house. Next week, or even next day snow whirls madly in circles over the meadow on a searing wind. It catches on the porch screens and in every little crevice. Odd noises that live in the chimney rumble to life. With a fine stippling sound flakes sweep the window glass. The following day a shining sun turns this white world into unbelievable beauty. Everything sparkles—the trees, the ground and even the air, as the sun catches flakes that are blowing.

January can be cold, clear nights with a racing wind and stars like slivered ice strewn across the sky. Mornings when we get up the temperature may be zero outside the living room window, or 19° or 20° below! Rhododendron leaves are curled tight into slim cigars. At sunrise a pink light glows behind the frosted trees fringing the meadow, a light that turns to dusty orange at sunset. The temperature hovers around zero all day. If the sun shines, things may melt a little and then the trees swing a million jewels along their branches.

January sunsets are spectacular. When the sun slips behind the trees flamboyant colors pour over the heavens—smokey orange, gold or scarlet. Soon lights brighten house windows, a horn sounds down the road, somewhere a dog barks and children call to one another in play. The first star appears, night falls.

Some time about the middle of January winter relaxes its grip and a great change occurs. The earth stirs briefly, turns and sleeps again. But in its stirring a few warm days take over. The air is soft. Melting snow runs rivers down the road, icicles on the eaves stream water, and rain gushes over the white meadow. January can be as changeable in its way and as temperamental as April. This annual thaw sends the first hint of sap up the trees and we gather pussy willows, forsythia branches, and a few lilac stems. We give them a lukewarm shower and in a week or so they begin to flower indoors. The lilac blossoms are miniature editions of their outdoor May blooms but no less charming.

Often we bring in branches of white birch and set them in a vase of water with good light but no direct sun. These not only unfold chartreuse leaves, but trail furry, jade-green catkins. One year a birch grove needed thinning and we cut off a tree about eight feet tall and not too broad at ground level. We brought this into the house during the January thaw and wired it upright in a large crock of water. In a couple of weeks the birch was leafing out and swinging catkins. Every hour something new seemed to happen on the little tree and it was exciting to observe the constant change.

After the drought last fall, I find my point of view about

rain somewhat different. I can never have too much. I love the sound and the look of it. In January it blows across the meadow in great billowing sheets of silver. If the temperature hovers at 32°, rain sounds like sand against the windows. I enjoy the peaceful interlude that a rainy day brings. And right now it is especially welcome with the reservoir low.

The willows turn gold, bare branches down by the stream are bright red, and tufts of meadow grass shoulder their way up through the melting snow. The temperature is 45°. I take a book and a blanket and sit in a protected spot outside the front door. The sun against the wall behind me sends out heat like a radiator.

Out by the mail boxes the tarred road is free of snow for the first time in weeks.

Walking along a tarred road, you travel a path of diamonds as the sun sparkles on slivers of mica in the tar. Water settles in the cracks where snow melts and the surface turns into a map of some mythical country. You find mountains, rivers, highways and cities. The road is also a contemporary design of mosaics. Trees send dark blue shadows over this road, and on a windy day they dance wildly.

In these unexpected warm days, "Never forget about spring," Nature is telling us. Spring always lies sleeping in the midst of winter, whether a winter of climate or a winter of the spirit. And now and then in January spring stirs to remind us of this heartening fact.

But spring is not really here. The dogwood buds are hard and round and secret. The hay-covered roses are a series of white humps and bumps in their bed, and there is ice in the wind that blows down inside your coat collar. Overnight the temperature drops, and you wake to a world of glass. The sun shines on the iced meadow and every small twig is frosted. As the day warms, bits of ice drop to the glare surface and slide down the slope to the brook or off toward the stone walls. Each bit of glass seeks its own path around nubbins of grass. Neighbor dogs have a time keeping upright. How surprised they are when their rear ends do not cooperate with their fore-legs. Now we enter the snow, sleet and ice age that also occurs in January. Birds need us for suet and seed as their ordinary food is encased in crystal. Icicles grow longer and longer on the eaves. By day their stiff sharp points drip in the sun. By night they freeze and lengthen.

My down-to-earth friend Hazel comes to tea.

"Icicles," she exclaimed when she entered the door, "hum!"

"Yes, aren't they beautiful," I said. "Come look." I led her to my favorite long ones. This cluster had sort of undulating circles at the top. One icicle had two legs like an overgrown garden carrot. Here another started as one, divided into two, then merged again at the bottom, forming a window. All were thick as Bull's-eye glass in Cape Cod houses.

"Hum," Hazel said. "If you have icicles dripping when it is below freezing, it usually means an insulation problem. You'd better get a roofer."

Hum indeed—I am reminded again by my friend that to keep ourselves in balance in this practical world we need both to appreciate icicles and to get the roofer. This is always a difficult role for me. Hazel is a good influence. Today I want only icicles, but tomorrow I will call the roofer.

Neither Bob nor I are exactly hermits but still we welcome the isolation that snow brings. It seems to snow every Friday night, thus leaving us snugly at home by the fire. Our planned dinner guests cannot get here, or we cannot get where we are supposed to be. The company surplus food goes into the freezer for the future. As long as the utilities work it is a treat at times to be freed from outside contacts and responsibilities. Our house becomes a small island.

These snowed-in week-ends become thoughtful days, days of a different kind of enjoyment. Psychologists speak of the value of withdrawal and return. We accept nature's withdrawal period as a valued gift. We read, and write letters to family and friends. Writing the children in the West and far-off friends is like a visit with them. We catch up on odd jobs around the house. At night Bob builds up a great fire and I hook my current rug while he reads.

We usually have some winter project under way. Last winter we were studying French. This year we are reading about England. At the moment we are deep in a book called *Katherine,* by Anya Seton. It deals with 14th century England, commoners in revolt, the Duke of Lancaster, feudal life, and the ravishingly beautiful Katherine Swynford. It is so exciting we can hardly wait to get through dinner and get the fire started. It is thick as a dictionary so we shall be there, back 600 years, for weeks. Let our friends bask at southern beaches, we don't envy them one little bit.

One night we were right in the throes of a revolution quite as gory as the French one with everyone cutting off everyone else's head, and carrying them (the heads) about on poles. Suddenly there was a great clap on our roof and we both jumped. It was a shock to be snapped so suddenly through 600 years to the present. And also, what could it be? The impact, though brief, sent a tremor through the house.

"Do you think it is a great goose flying against the roof overhead?" I asked Bob.

"Wrong season for wild geese," he replied, "besides geese aren't that dumb."

It had been almost rough enough to crack the windows. We were mystified but since nothing further occurred, Bob added another log and we slid blissfully back to the 14th century.

Next morning at breakfast, Bob said, "I'll bet it was a plane breaking the sound barrier we heard last night."

What a contrast to 14th century England when transportation was by horseback or on foot. We have come a long way in these 600 years and not only as far as transportation and science are concerned. We have a friend who is convinced that there never was so much evil in the world as there is today. As I read about the 14th century, the beheadings, the poisonings, the treachery, and casual disregard for human life, I do not believe this is true. The quality of relationships between people has vastly changed and improved. Human life today has considerably more value and a different value. There are still evil men and evil actions and probably always will be. But today there is a public conscience which condemns these things. In our lifetime we've seen the concentration camps of the last war, and other terrible things closer to home, but we also see the forces of national and international government being directed towards correcting them. Certainly there is more innate goodness in governments and individuals today, more balance and just plain sense of humanity of man for man.

January is the month we have paper-white narcissus blooming in the house. I've often bought fancy ones from elite garden centers at fancy prices and found them rather indifferent in their performance. This last fall I neglected to send away for them. Shopping one day in Food Fair my eye was caught by a forgotten plastic bag with five bulbs in it on the back of a shelf. All had begun to grow. Green sprouts, emerging from the bulb tips, were curving up inside the plastic. This urge for life won me. How could I pass them by? When I got home I arranged the bulbs in pebbles and water and covered the tops with a brown paper bag. I stood them under the greenhouse bench and forgot them. I filled the dish with water every couple of weeks. Today I took off the bag and there they are, a foot high and in bud. They occupy a place of honor on the dining room table, and already the scent from one little opening narcissus fills the room. On top of the piano stand sprays of just-opening forsythia. In the kitchen window over the sink birch leaves and catkins are forming. Orchids are flowering in the greenhouse, and bright red geraniums.

This day is important to Bob and me. Six weeks ago we each decided to lose twelve pounds. Tonight on the scale we have achieved our goals—we are each twelve pounds lighter.

We both feel like a million, have twice as much energy, and we do look quite different. It was all so easy, pleasant and full of surprises.

For the last year I have slowly but surely been gaining weight, and most of it around the middle. At first I hesitated to diet because reducing diets can not only be complicated but also difficult, and because I like to eat. But the main reason was, I am not a Spartan character. Chocolate malted milk shakes are my joy and delight.

However, early in December I tried on my favorite evening dress for a holiday party and it wouldn't fit. That did it for me. One night after dinner when Bob went to relax in an easy chair, he found that, to be comfortable, he had to loosen his belt. This he said, was his turning point.

Once the decision was made, nothing would stop us. We resolved not to talk about it, but just to do it. My husband weighed 172. His goal was 160. I weighed 132. My goal was 120. There are, I suspect, about as many systems of losing weight as there are flowers in a meadow—the cottage cheese method, the lamb chop and pineapple school, the eat fat and grow thin way, and a seven day diet that starves you the first day with only two bran muffins. But our method is uncomplicated, natural, rewarding. In fact, our way is so simple that people scarcely pay any attention when we tell them about it.

WE ATE LESS.

We ate almost everything we liked, but less, literally less food on the plate than would completely fill us up. We'd have two strips of bacon instead of four, a small baked potato instead of a large one. We took no seconds. We skipped desserts most of the time or else had small amounts of fruit.

Little did I dream of the innumerable side effects of losing weight. We were both moving about more easily and lightly on our feet. Merely carrying around less weight could have a lot to do with this. All that six weeks the rewards were stupendous. We met them in the mirror, in the comments of friends, and in an exhilarating sense of well being.

The first twenty-four hours we each lost two pounds. We continued to lose at the rate of about two pounds a week. One day at the home of a friend we encountered spoon bread served with melted butter sauce. The fragrance alone was devastating. I could practically feel my character form as I took only a small helping, but I could also feel it shattering as I contemplated a second. However, when Bob refused a second, that settled it.

Thinking back, I never needed to grit my teeth and exercise will power. When at first I felt a slight hunger pang, a glass of water or a stick of fresh, crisp celery usually solved it. If not, I thought of that unwanted roll of fat and how, at this very moment, it was melting away. Most of the diet books, helpful as they may be, give you a schedule and a discipline from the outside. When you decide to lose by eating less, you embark upon a different kind of discipline—one that occurs from the inside. Reaching your goal this way brings a special satisfaction.

Two basic requirements for success in losing weight by our method are, (1) the will to do it, (2) the willingness to eat less. If the first requirement is there, the second follows easily.

To celebrate our twelve-pound loss, I am planning to bake an apple pie for company dinner tomorrow, and if we have a blizzard it can go in the freezer! But whenever we do serve it, we'll eat less of it than we would have a few months ago. And, because of this, we shall, I now know, enjoy it more.

During this last six weeks, especially at first, I have often said, "Wait till I lose those pounds, and as a reward I'm going to eat a large sundae—vanilla ice cream, chocolate sauce, malted milk powder, nuts, whipped cream, oh yes, and a cherry!"

"You'd better lose two extra pounds before that one," Bob laughed.

Now the time has come for my revel. But a strange thing has occurred. My fabulous sundae is a lovely thought and probably some time I shall have a small scale one and enjoy it tremendously but I don't feel I have to have one today. Nobody could be more surprised than I at such a turn of events!

That morning though I may have walked down to the box for the mail, I certainly floated back. I always love to see Bob Jr.'s broad, open, generous handwriting on one of his long envelopes, with a San Francisco postmark. And there it lay on top of everything. My fingers were slightly freezing while I stood there opening it, but I couldn't wait.

"Dear Ma and Pa," it began. "Susan and Miles and I are coming east to pay you a visit in May, if this would be a good time." I was so excited at this point I couldn't see the rest of the letter. My only companions for sharing this great news with was a small chickadee on a nearby hemlock branch, our next door ten-year-old walking by on his way home from school, and a telephone repair man enclosed in a white tent on top of a pole.

I'm sure my feet never touched the ground all the way home. As soon as I got in the house I called Bob Sr., at his office. I had finally calmed down enough to read the rest of the letter and discover that they would be staying three weeks. Miles is not quite three and we haven't seen him since he was a scrambling rosy-cheeked baby who laughed one minute and screamed the next, constantly wiggled, and cuddled wherever and whenever possible. His curiosity about all of life had known no bounds. He also played endlessly with some "blocks" made from all sizes of empty food cans which Bob and Susan had scrubbed and filed so they had no dangerous edges. He never tired of rolling these about, piling them up, or fitting them inside each other. Their gay labels were so very colorful. Susan is an artist and ingenious. I always thought her invention a most creative plaything for a child.

And now in the best month of the year and one of the loveliest in our garden and meadow we were to have this small family with us. A true cause for celebration. All the rest of that day, through every activity I felt an undercurrent of pure delight.

Bob had a meeting that evening. He stays in Rye for the night when there is an evening activity, so I was alone. We had shared our joy over the phone and by late afternoon I was calm and collected once more.

I have a wonderful way of spending evenings alone. It might not suit everyone, but it completely pleases me. Reading in bed is one of my favorite pastimes, and so is eating red grapes in winter. I never have quite enough of either. When alone I have dinner about four-thirty. By five or five-thirty I am comfortably settled in bed with a nice lot of pillows and a bunch of grapes. I have three or more hours at a stretch. This is enough time to be really transported to the scene of my book or its era. I am usually reading about far places, or years ago, or both. By eight or nine I am off to sleep and I sleep the clock around.

Tonight my reading took a different direction, I was lifted into the realm of philosophy and psychology by Carl Rogers in his book *On Becoming a Person*. So much is written these days about improving ourselves, the implication being that there is something wrong with us as we are. It is easy to identify with the weaknesses and faults you read about and first thing you know you're off in about ten different directions at one time, IMPROVING. So often in these articles and books the emphasis tends to be on what is lacking. I'm all for changing and growing but lately I have been hoping that just once somebody would write about what is *right with us* instead of what is wrong. I was pleased to find in part of Carl Rogers' book material dealing with the normal, balanced, sound and solid individual, and what some of his characteristics are—what is "right with him." Professor Rogers was referring to the person who is emotionally healthy, who is fulfilling himself, using his talents and abilities, and doing about the best he is capable of doing.

It was pleasant to recognize a great many of these traits in our friends and, happily, a few in myself. I'm sure we grow just as much and maybe more by being aware and amplifying what is good about us as by stirring and muddying up the depth of what is wrong. Sometimes while you are working with good traits you inadvertently find yourself shedding some bad ones. Certain faults simply drop away without your realizing it, or sometimes you find you have grown beyond them.

From Rogers I gleaned that when you are living the good and fulfilled life, you are constantly in a process and never in a static state of having arrived anywhere. I always tend to do something and then say, "there" in a final sort of way. But in this business of growing I guess you just keep on and on.

Those who are leading a fulfilled life, Professor Rogers goes on to say, are open and interested in new experiences, outwardly and inwardly. They are alert to feelings in themselves and others of courage, tenderness and awe, and also feelings of fear and discouragement. In a word, they shut nothing out. They are not afraid to be afraid. The sound, solid person lives increasingly in each moment knowing that the next moment can only grow out of the present one. He lives in the main with a feeling of safety, of being accepted, loved, and of loving. Certain of his roots are finding nourishment in some kind of philosophy or religion. He can listen, really listen, and with love and interest, to another and also to himself. He is a good judge of character and usually recognizes the spurious and artificial. He never tries to impress others with his importance. He is completely at home in the world of Nature. This last, of course, particularly intrigued me.

How delightful to learn also that the balanced individual is often inaccurate, untidy, vague, and unconventional, and does things on the spur of the moment. This was quite comforting as I can be all of these at times, and thoroughly.

Bob Jr. had started off this perfect day, and Carl Rogers provided its final note. I turned out the light about eight in a contented frame of mind feeling I knew a number of normal, balanced people in and out of the family.

My mind then returned to the news of the day. I began visualizing Bob Jr., Susan, Miles and Bob Sr. and me all flying our new Persian kite down at Compo Beach. I wonder with five hundred yards of string if we will be lifted off the ground too. It might be rather fun to soar over the beach and have a gull's eye view of the Westport coastline.

Of course, there are a number of weeks before May—and winter weeks. Perhaps during these I will waken some moonlight night and find that herd of fifty white-tailed deer grazing outside the window. Then I will awaken Bob and probably telephone all the neighbors too! I drifted off to sleep with the thought that I must remember to look in the almanac and see when the moon would next be full.

2

February is blue ice and deep snow

FEBRUARY IS THE VERY HEART of winter. Snow swirls tree-top high while skiers in flying red scarves weave patterns over rolling hillsides, and red-mittened neighbor children build snowmen in their front yards. Temperatures tumble and hover for days around zero or below. A north wind blows, obviously off the icebergs. Up and down the valley, through the cold, clear air you hear the rising and falling cadences of a power saw at work—a sure sound of winter. Our woodpile grows larger and so do those of the neighbors. When we walk around the reservoir in the late afternoons, we hear the mysterious voice of the ice. This ice, humped up around stumps and rocks along the shore, melts a little during the day. In freezing again at dusk it sends occasional haunting echoes through the hills.

These are weeks of fires, and friends, and indoor life. February is the scent of freshly ironed handkerchiefs in the kitchen on a gray and snowy day. February is beef stew for dinner and the fun of preparing the vegetables, shiny onions, firm potatoes, rich orange carrots, and crisp celery, then smelling the delectable aroma of simmering stew all afternoon. With freezing fingers I delve into the bushel basket of sand in the garage for our home-grown carrots. How good they are. Each one has a tiny, pale gold, new leaf beginning to grow at the top. They are alive there in the cold sand.

One morning after Bob left I sat down by the window to watch the birds. A mere bunch of feathers on a twig might not seem so very significant in the overall picture, but it is. According to our bird book one single chickadee devoured a hundred-and-thirty-eight thousand cankerworm eggs in twenty-five days! Aside from their general usefulness at every season, it's a joy to feed birds during the winter. In a blizzard we are literally a lifeline to these lovely creatures. You get to know the different kinds and sometimes certain birds themselves. One particular chickadee is my friend. Each day I'm especially pleased when he comes for his sunflower seed. He perches near me while I scatter food.

Our feeders are only fifteen feet from the window and binoculars bring the birds practically into my lap. The perky little sparrow with the black dot on his fluffy breast is a tree sparrow, and the one with no dot is a field sparrow. I often mix these up. The lady junco has touches of brown. The male is charming with his slate gray head and back, and creamy undersides. The nuthatch is another winner. He creeps cheerfully down the maple trunk head first. Sometimes his world is upside down, sometimes right side up. He views it with equanimity either way. With a long bill he reaches out, quickly snatches a seed, and flies off. The markings of the nuthatch are the essence of winter. His blues and grays are the mists that drift over the meadow and brush against Pop's Mountain at dusk. The golden tans on his underside are wisps of dried grass in the meadow, beech leaves in the woods with sun shining on them, or last year's oak leaves that still cling.

The gentleman cardinal hops about the ground picking up food and feeding his lady who preens herself at being thus cherished. In the feeders the cardinal has precedence. The others respect his rights, and move aside. Through the binoculars I can see the bright, beady eyes of all the visitors and watch the breeze ruffle their feathers. Each bird out there in the cold encompasses a whole world of instincts and nature's rhythms. Every one fits into the general scheme with his purposes and his destiny. Even empty birds' nests provide snug winter hybernating places for bumblebees and other small insects. Out our north window an oriole nest swings high in an elm. What a cozy winter a family of bumblebees could spend there.

Birds are constantly doing mysterious things. Why did the bluebirds appear last week for two or three days and then take off again for who knows where? They do this several times every winter. Why do the black crows come to our south meadow late this month at 6 a.m. and fill the air with loud cawing, and again at the end of August, same time, same place? Does some special delicacy sprout there or ripen at these times?

We may never learn the answers of these and half a dozen other questions. But one thing we do discover as bird watchers and bird feeders, our own awareness continually develops and sharpens, and along with it our sense of wonder.

That morning as I watched the birds a strange thing occurred. All at once, in a split second, and for no visible reason, every single bird dropped to the ground and seemed to disappear. What could this be? I saw no neighboring dog or cat. While some had scurried to the walls, the rest had slid up to the feeder posts or to humps of meadow grass, and a few scuttled out of sight in the ground ivy. Wherever they were they remained still as statues, and reminded me of a game I used to play as a child called "Still Pond, No More Moving." Then I saw the cause of it all. Circling above the treetops, small as a distant plane, was a bird, probably a hawk. He was so high I couldn't be sure, and yet the birds knew. How well they knew! Had they seen his shadow? Even after the hawk had flown off, for several minutes there was not a move among them.

Our feeders, and we have two groups of three, are a little bit unusual. One summer we were driving through Blue Earth, Minnesota, and we bought some harrow discs in a junk yard for twenty-five cents each. Bob painted and mounted each one on a cedar post with one end sunk in the ground. Every feeder stands at a slightly different height and they look like a cluster of Alice-in-Wonderland mushrooms.

A harrow disc comes with a hole in the center. This was covered with a piece of screening so rain would run out and leave the birdseed dry. Harrow discs have a graceful curve and make fine feeders. They can be acquired readily in any rural area. When anyone uses a harrow, discs need replacing and old ones become available. Ours are painted yellow to match the trim on the house. I'll never forget how one day in one of these rich gold discs we had, and at the same time, a purple finch, a bright yellow goldfinch, a cardinal, and a blue jay. To cap the climax, an indigo bunting suddenly arrived, and as quickly, departed. I have never seen this rare and beautiful little bird before or since.

Today the birds are brilliant against the snow. In a June world of green and vivid summer flowers, cardinals and blue jays merge into the general color scheme, but in winter against snow, both are arresting and invite particular attention. Snow causes all colors to appear more brilliant. Surely the hemlocks by the walls are greener today, the pines and laurel, too. It is almost as if snow launders all colors and sends them to our vision span clean and sparkling. Snow also simplifies and eliminates clutter in the landscape, so we have less to look at. Perhaps what we do see, as a consequence, appears sharper and clearer.

This is the time of year we are drawn to bright colors everywhere, indoors and out. I'm embroidering some pillows, little patchwork patterns made of old silk neckties. Fancy embroidery stitches join the pieces together. It is a pleasure to work with and to look at this rainbow of embroidery yarns in my basket, and the bright shapes of the silk ties.

My eyes linger on all the vivid colors in the living room. The red and yellow books on the shelves, curtains, cushions, pictures, and, of course, the flowers in the greenhouse. We have orchids in all colors blooming this month, and the dusty pink blooms of Aurora Borealis are unfolding beside a huge ruby-red trumpet of amaryllis. Red is a color of particular appeal at this season. It is the first primary color, and in ancient symbolism represented the earth. Today, as then, it suggests life, vigor, and energy. No wonder we are drawn to it when outside all visible life is at a pause. In a certain month we are attracted to one color, and in another mood to another. In midwinter we want all the brightest to wear and to live with.

In a north window African violets thrive and bring us their brilliant tints. Did you ever look at an African violet flower closely? The rich velvety blue is a magnificent tone, and the bloom itself a work of art and well worth studying with a magnifying glass. Notice not only the petals but the miniature gold pinheads at the center and the single blue hair curving out of the heart to stand guard over the yellow parts. African violet leaves are also charming with their delicate "fur." They feel wonderful to touch, almost as pleasant as my favorite "stroking plant," Siderasis Fuscata, with its leaves downy on both sides.

February air has a flavor all its own. It is not only crisp and cold and tingles in your nose when you go walking, but something more. We hear a lot about spring air, summer air, and that of autumn. But do pause briefly and appreciate the air that nature sends us in midwinter. Open the door and take a breath. The "flavor" is fresh and distinctive and you can almost taste it. After a few moments you feel invigorated and satisfied. House air, however fresh, is different. Experiments have proven that the air in the average home in winter is drier than the Sahara Desert. Even without this somewhat ominous fact, house air at this time of year lacks something. I'm sure we're fed and nourished by many things in addition to food —by colors, by things we touch, *and* by icy cold outdoor February air.

On a windless, sunny morning I took some pillows outside to replenish them. Fresh covers were needed and additional down which I would transfer from an old down quilt. Down is remarkable—deliciously soft, snowy white, and alive. You stuff it in a pillow, and it doesn't stay but emerges to drift about with a will of its own. I and the down became intimately acquainted. I remembered the fairy tale of the princess who went down the well after her golden shuttle and met Mother Hulla airing and shaking her down puff to make a snowstorm on earth. I created a real blizzard out there on the terrace with myself in the eye of the storm. A few hours later I came in with three brand new handsome pillows *and* with down all over me. I'm sure my black sweater will never be the same again. Whisks of down blew over the terrace until it looked as if somebody had knitted the bricks together. I got it in my hair, I was breathing it, it caught on my eyelashes. That night there was a wisp in the soup, and in the book I was reading. For several days we found down in the oddest places, inside shoes, in the shower, on my toothbrush. And stray bits came gently over the floor everywhere to greet us. But it was great to get such nice new pillows. It is always satisfying to use up what you have, or turn it into something else. That useless old quilt had been stuffed way back in the linen closet and came to light in last month's cleaning spree. Homemade down pillows are like anything homemade—just a little bit better, and, of course, created to your own desires. These were full and puffy and so soft.

The bathroom is filled with Jim Moore painting a beautiful terra cotta color on the wall—not that Jim is so large, but the room is small. For fifteen years we have had our original colors in the house and we decided to have a little painting done. Our idea was to capture the color of these dramatic winter sunsets. The bathroom was a dusky eggplant tone and Bob thought burnt orange would be a nice change. The room is north and can take a warm color.

"Jim, we'd like the walls the shade of the recent sunsets, but a little less passionate. Could you do this, do you think?" I asked.

"You know," he replied, "we can't see the sunsets from our house, so I'm not sure what you mean." But he brought in from his car a whole covey of little paint cans, spread them on newspapers, and the fun began.

Too light, too dark, too pink, too green, too red, too brown. Then, all of a sudden, there is a beautiful color. I don't know if it would match a local sunset, but it is a color that appeals to Bob and me.

Jim says our sunset idea reminds him of the time a woman asked him to mix a color for her bedroom and match a spray of apple blossoms that she had in her hand.

"Did you ever look at one of those blossoms?" Jim asked. "Every petal is different." He shook his head. "That was something, I'm telling you. But then I never was asked to do a wall like a sunset before," he added, ruminating and flexing his clean brush.

Jim is the man who painted our house in the first place, and who has mixed colors for us ever since. It is with a great bucket of his mix that Bob is now covering the outside of the house.

It was a pleasure to have Jim around. He always had an

amusing story to tell. There was his painter friend who was given a sample on a cardboard to match. The lady client (apparently we ladies are the problem) then took off for the day. The man had trouble getting the tone so he mixed the color as closely as he could, painted the walls, and then painted the sample, too. When the lady of the house returned, she looked at both wall and sample and said, "Well, I don't know how you ever got such a perfect match."

One day while Jim was eating the lunch he always brings we were talking about birds.

"Did you ever get near one of those whippoorwills at night?" he asked.

"No, did you?"

"I sure did, and did you know, they have red eyes! Those night fliers never make a wing sound, you know, and we were walking once, Peg and I. I thought this bird was going to get caught in her hair, he flew so close, we saw his eyes clearly and they are red as coals."

For a week the smell of paint filled the house. One thing about Jim, he's the neatest painter I ever knew. He never gets a drop of paint where it shouldn't be. You leave in the morning, return at night and a ceiling is painted and you'd never know anyone had been in the room.

We had the woodwork in my bedroom done, all the ceilings, every day a different one, and the bathroom. This gave the house a brand new, fresh and clean look.

And now in the terra cotta bathroom the curtains are an English cotton print, several shades of deep green and a few touches of yellow. The new handsome green shower curtain is the color of summer sunlight on maple leaves.

February days are growing visibly longer. A dozen or so crocuses are out on the south side of the terrace along the house where it is protected. In their unfolding yellow petals these flowers catch and hold a sun that is brighter and warmer. The sun is different this month. In January it is silver-white but in February it is touched with gold. Sometimes we waken to the slightly hesitant but lilting music of the cardinal's first song, and over the meadow a mourning dove sings at dusk. We enjoy these brief hints of the shape of things to come. Spring is not here, not even imminent, but it sends a welcome promise.

Meanwhile, what a lovely Valentine's week-end! We woke Saturday to a perfect morning, clear, crisp and cold. After breakfast we set out for Brookside Nursery in Darien to get the report of our soil that Mr. Bullpit did last fall. We would then buy the organic plant food needed to put everything in proper balance.

The report had been basically good but we were low on minerals. Mr. Bullpit filled the car with bags of organic raw bone meal, aerosoil (a lime formula soil conditioner), cotton hull ash (a potash supply), and Nature's Nutrients, a good general mix for everything. The rear end of the car was so heavy that we had the sensation of steering a motorboat as we swayed up the Parkway. Bob seemed to have confidence in the springs, though, so I decided I might as well relax.

"What a garden we'll have this year," I exclaimed as our rear swerved slightly to the left with a kind of a liquid roll.

"Things will certainly grow rampantly and sky high," Bob replied, guiding us skillfully back to our side of the road.

This slightly swaying car motion lulled me into a dreamy mood.

"We'll have our own personal Jack's beanstalk," I commented, and began envisioning little rows of golden crook-necked squash hanging in circles around the rims of small cumulus clouds and a fringe of cucumbers transforming a slim veil of another cloud into a comb.

Right after lunch we put on galoshes and headed for the garden to spread the fertilizer and relieve the car of its great load. Even if spring was only a promise, it was pleasant to be doing something related to the planting season ahead.

Piles of snow at the garden edges had to be negotiated to

get into the area, but in an hour or so, we scattered about 800 pounds of organic food. Such a grand feeling to see the gray powder with its vital life-giving qualities over our snow-covered earth. Organic fertilizer can go on weeks ahead of planting since it is slow in action. The ground was solidly frozen so it was easy to push the wheelbarrow. The powder grayed my hair, and we breathed in so many minerals that we shouldn't need vitamins for days. The rains and snows of the next month or six weeks will carry all this down in. Our next summer's vegetables will not only have a proper and balanced diet, but will contain more health-giving minerals for us. We go along with the organic gardeners who believe that adding natural minerals (rather than synthetic ones) to the soil benefits not only the vegetables grown there, but the people who eat them.

An interesting and scientifically controlled experiment was recently made on lettuce. The same lettuce seed was planted in three different batches of identical soil. Care and watering for all three was the same. One was given no fertilizer, one commercial fertilizer, one organic fertilizer. When the heads developed a chemical analysis showed the protein content of the organically fed lettuce to be a good deal higher. In the other two it was about the same.

You can get into very hot arguments on this subject with non-organic gardeners. We find it best to keep quiet.

The favorite argument of the anti-organic people is, "How does a small root know the difference between organic calcium and chemical calcium? It just wants calcium. Calcium is calcium, so there."

But there is a difference. Organic foods build up the soil itself, slowly, and over a long period. They increase the earth's bacterial content and its general vitality. Needed food elements are there and remain there waiting for roots to select what they need *when* they need it, and a little at a time. Many commercial fertilizers merely toss food at plants in great amounts whether they are ready for it or not. Nothing happens basically to improve the soil in a lasting way, and the fertilizer does not remain in the earth long.

Our garden should be better than ever, we both agreed, as we emptied the last of the bags and shook out our jackets.

That evening we settled by the fire to order seeds.

"We should have something brand new and mysterious, don't you think?" I asked Bob. "Besides, you like oysters."

We were sitting on the sofa, each of us with a Burpee catalogue in hand.

"What are you talking about?" said Bob, who doesn't like to have his train of thought interrupted. "And what have oysters to do with ordering vegetables?" he asked vaguely, writing down 'Tendergreen String Beans, one-half pound—95¢.'

"Oyster Plant," I said.

"Never heard of it."

"Neither did I."

"Where is it?" Bob asked.

"Page 38. Do let's try it."

"Okay, but wait till we get there. We're only in the B's—Beans," Bob said.

I often think I must have been Chinese in some previous incarnation because I always want to operate backwards. In adding the checkbook I tend to begin at the end and work towards the beginning, which can cause quite a lot of arithmetic confusion. With seed catalogues I have the same inclination. I open at the end, or in the middle, or anywhere, but seldom at the beginning. This drives Bob slightly mad. It's wonderful to have his sound and logical nature to keep me going in a somewhat forward direction.

So there we were in beans, golden and green ones, lush and crisp on the page. The fire crackled, the outside temperature was 10 above and what better way to spend that February evening than in sending off our annual order.

We chose and selected right through the book from beans

to zucchini. Bob listed the order for mailing and I listed the same order in our garden notebook. This latter is one of the most valuable items in our horticultural lives. It is a small, spiral-bound book in which we write down every item of particular interest related to the garden. All seeds bought are listed, dates purchased, dates planted, and the date that each crop matures. First crocuses and all firsts of special interest go in the book, and all costs.

Anything particularly thrilling that happens is also recorded, like our 96 cucumbers in one month from three hills. Anything terrible is also noted, like the cankerworms all over everything and how we solved them by banding the trees with Tanglefoot, and the next year never had a one. This book is a wonderful reference work.

We studied last year's vegetable list and decided what had been unusually good. These items we would reorder. If something hadn't been excellent we would change the variety.

We pored over pages of bright red tomatoes whose juice practically ran off the page, lush cantaloupes that we can never grow, try as we will. I could practically taste the sweet corn as I looked at the realistic ears of Honey-Cross Bantam. I was thinking of our freezer-full that we'd been enjoying all winter.

The Dwarf Extra Curled Parsley all but curls off into my lap, and how crisp the Salad Bowl Lettuce is—and here is the Oyster Plant, "Salsify" it is also called.

"Shall we try it?" I asked.

It lies across the page, three pure white carrot-like shapes.

"It looks odd, but if you like," said Bob, good-naturedly writing it down. He is soon lost in the peas on the next page, peas, and peas, and peas.

Of course we must grow turnips, sixty days. The purpletops are delicious. Last year we let them stay in the ground too long and they were woody. It was the first time we had planted them. This year we will remember to harvest them sooner. So there is the order, ready to mail in the morning.

Bob goes out for an apple and I to the kitchen for my recent discovery of hot milk and molasses.

At the Country Emporium in West Redding, where they specialize in superb pancakes in ten different flavors, we first met this molasses. It comes by the barrel with a pump in the top, and stands just beyond the pot-bellied stove next to the raspberry, strawberry, and blueberry syrups. You take your own container and Mr. Tree starts to pump. After a few interesting squeals and grunts, rich, dark molasses begins to flow out the spout to fill the gallon glass jug.

This molasses is without peer, incomparable, unsulphured, uneverythinged. Pure and delicious. A tablespoon stirred into a cup of hot milk at night is ambrosia and a perfect going-to-bed drink for a cold winter night.

Watching the last embers in the grate, Bob ate his crisp apple and I sipped my drink. Something about winter fires draws the conversation along intimate lines. Different kinds of thoughts prosper when there is a cold winter wind in the trees and at the windows, and warmth and companionship within. Words are perhaps fewer but more significant and thoughts move on a different level. Winter provides time for us to know better those with whom we live closely. It provides time to explore our own inner natures, and become better acquainted with our own thinking. How rewarding it becomes then to share some of these discoveries with someone who is understanding.

After turning out the lights we were drawn to the large window by a brightness. A full moon shone on the meadow. I wondered where the white-tailed deer were tonight. By any chance would they come?

It was beautiful outside. Shadows cast by moonlight weave their own magic, and dancing over the snow, cast their spell. Moonlight was streaming over a garden where seeds will sprout and grow, where vegetables will nourish and fragrant flowers bloom. It seemed to me as I stood looking out that many of the things we get all stirred up about have less value in the overall pattern than the sight of a full moon shining down on a sleeping garden, or tangled up in the bare branches of a maple tree along a stone wall.

It was one of those sunny mornings that is a state of mind as well as a kind of weather. Our grandson Jesse was coming the following day for a week's visit. As soon as Bob left, I started cooking. Jesse is fourteen and his appetite insatiable. Bob and he both love apple pie, so I began there. While the pie was in process I made a coconut custard and while that was in the works, I cooked some wheat and soya cereal—rather like the old-fashioned Wheatena, only better. All the while chicken bones were simmering into soup on the back of the stove. Whenever I had a new idea, I'd add something else, such as celery, parsley, onion, left-over carrots, lettuce leaves, a green pepper.

The washing machine was humming along finishing up the laundry. The sound of the utilities working is always a pleasant one to hear. It's good to have everything caught up when Jesse arrives, then I can have a holiday as well as give him one. He or Jeff come every year at this time for their mid-winter vacation. Probably that is partly why it was such a sunny day indoors and out.

Leaving the pie and custard in the oven I walked down the road to get the mail and a mile or so further with the dogs. Bingo lives across the brook to our right and Gypsy lives across the lane to our left. They meet on our place and romp and play together endlessly. When thoroughly exhausted they stretch out side by side under the apple tree and contemplate the meadow scene. When I went out the door neither one was in sight. Those dogs must be psychic! They are nowhere visible but as soon as I walked fifty feet, there they both are and I have an escort. We three have a comfortable relationship, friendly but independent. We start out together, but sometimes they wander farther and I come home alone.

It was cold and windy and the trees squeaked as they do

in midwinter when the wind blows. My face felt icy cold and stiff that morning, and I was reminded of an incident from my childhood. My older sister and I were driving the horse and buggy to the store for groceries. My hands were snug and warm inside my muff, but my face was so cold I began to cry. I kept telling her how I was sure it was really going to freeze.

Connie said cheerfully, "You'd better stop crying then and smile because it would be terrible to have to go all through life with a crying expression frozen on your face."

My toes and fingers felt tingly when I came back in the house and the kitchen was pleasantly fragrant with the aroma of pie and custard.

How much a child in his teens grows each year. Last year we were frying marbles in a hot iron skillet to watch the fascinating patterns that form in the center of the glass ones after they roll around a while in a hot iron pan. But this year is first year high school and the volume of a sphere is 4/3 *of pi-R-cubed,* and the area of a *sphere is 4 times pi-R squared,* and we have to borrow a neighbor's compass for making circles. I don't know whether we are trying to race with Russia or what inspires teachers to give children homework during their holidays, but I'm against it.

Usually I walk up through the glen sedately on the road, but not this week. Jesse finds a path that leads down over the boulders thirty feet below to where the water madly foams in torrents around the rocks. He climbs in and out of potholes while we shout to one another above the pounding flume. Jesse tosses rocks on the ice and if they don't crack it he decides we can walk safely. We discover a grotto of blue ice and all around outside great columns stand like huge organ pipes. We pause before a slim tube of blue-white ice. Next to it is a cluster, like a group of nuns, in long white robes with folded coifs, and here a comb of icicles fringes the rocky ledge. All these icicles are as blue as the inside of a glacier. For years I've passed these same fluted walls where the water cascades over cliffs and freezes but this is the first time they were ever blue —and they really *are* blue.

Black water tumbles and tears along sending an icy spray in our faces as we climb from rock to rock. High above is the road where safe and sane people walk, where grandmothers without a visiting grandson walk. But we are in the center of things and somewhat awed by the splendor of rocks and ice, and the force of the water. For a moment the splendor, the rocks, the ice and we seemed all of a piece. Listening to the roaring water, I received, and I think Jesse did too, the message of the river—a message that has been here for hundreds of years and will be here for hundreds more.

"Grandma, all those letters and pictures up in the attic—can I go up and look through them?"

Jesse brings down bundles of old letters. He discovers newspapers of World War II, a small box of our wedding cake which is definitely undesirable these many years later. He finds our old wedding picture. I remember the occasion as being an extremely gay and happy one, but in the photograph all of us, bridesmaids and ushers alike, looked more like a funeral than a wedding, not a shadow of a smile amongst us. Jesse brought down one real treasure, a log kept by his great-great-grandfather on a sailing vessel in which he went from Providence to Mobile, Alabama. It took three weeks and cost the sum of $30.00. All that evening Bob read it aloud. The marvelous spidery handwriting with s's like f's took us back 130 years. As David approached Alabama, Bob and Jesse were down on the floor plotting his course in the atlas and we all had a fascinating trip.

Some evenings we played Marble Out, a sort of combined version of Chinese Checkers and Parcheesi, or we played three-part music on our recorders. Jesse was planning to build a desk and was measuring ours. It is a real old one and has, on one side, a mark made by the wheel of the cart that carried it through a move long years ago. While I hooked my unicorn rug, Bob and Jesse had long discussions and figurings on paper about lumber and measurements.

Even drying the dishes during the week of Jesse's visit

had a new dimension. One evening Jesse flicked an aluminum pot cover with his thumb and forefinger.

"What is this note, Grandpa?"

Now we are flicking all the aluminum pot covers in the drawer to see which one is what note. All are a little different. Some sharper, some flatter. I can't pick the note but Jesse and Bob are often able to.

I took Jesse to the Modern Museum in New York City. He had never been. I was amazed at his receptiveness to contemporary art. We both became terribly excited by an exhibition on the ground floor. In each "picture" on the wall there was some kind of motion, slow motion. One was a wall of bricks, and the bricks undulated ever so slightly as if something were trying to break through from behind, first here, then there. Another was a mixture of colors and stars moving about in the way that suggested the creation of the universe. How could we ever leave? For a long time we didn't.

It was refreshing to see again our favorites among the Impressionists, too. We sat a while in the room with Cézanne's *Rocks and Pines,* Degas' *Ballet Dancers,* and Van Gogh's *Starry Night,* and, of course, my other favorite, Rousseau's *Sleeping Gypsy.* The colors of the gypsy's robe seem brighter each visit. We also lingered with Monet's *Water Lilies.* You can always match your mood of the moment to some part of this masterpiece.

While Jesse was gazing in rapt attention at the lilies, there passed between us something strangely akin to the feeling we had had down in the gorge mutually appreciating ice. I was aware of a special kind of sharing that comes when, with someone you love, you respond to a great work of art or to some aspect of nature. For a brief instant you touch something together—something greater than each of you would experience alone.

One day that week I took Jesse skating at the rink. While we were driving down Valley Forge Road in a snowstorm, he asked:

"Grandma, have you ever had any adventures?"

"Adventures?" I answered vaguely peering through the windshield and trying to see where the road was in the rapidly descending snow.

"Yes, you know, like fighting Indians."

I suppose I do seem ancient to a fourteen-year-old but I was hardly prepared to think of myself as belonging to that era.

"Well, no, Jesse," I said, "no Indians, but I do remember climbing a volcano in Guatemala some years ago," I said somewhat absently. I was trying to figure out if that looming shadow ahead was a truck, a telephone pole, or the river.

At the word volcano Jesse sparked into great life and enthusiasm. "Do tell me about that volcano, Grandma," he glowed and, with a contented wiggle, settled back in his seat.

The snow flakes were like loosely put together viburnum blossoms. You couldn't see ten feet ahead and I was thinking nostalgically of the warm house and pleasant fire we had left and wondering how Bob would ever be able to drive home from Rye that night.

Jesse had one eye out the window on the blizzard and the other on me while I did my best to recall our experience of fifteen years ago climbing the volcano Pacaya with a guide and a string of donkeys. I particularly remembered the joy of running down the outside of the cone. It was rather like sliding down a sand dune barefoot. You would take one step and slip three. Way high up there, with Guatemala City a scattering of white pin-pricks in the distance below, it was somewhat like flying. The difference between this and running down a sand dune, however, was that you wore heavy boots and you were ankle deep in volcanic ash which is like finely ground cinders. I got quite worked up myself remembering it all and forgot for the moment our snail's pace through the blowing snow, and our inability to see ahead.

I was telling Jesse how our guide had tethered the donkeys and baked eggs for our lunch in a steamy volcano pocket at the summit, and how the rim on which we sat to eat them was quite hot. With a little embroidery it made quite a good tale, and Jesse was spellbound. I had just about got us off the volcano when we reached the Post Road.

All over the place cars were abandoned, others were slithering across the road from side to side or were just plain stuck in the middle. If I'd had any sense at all and hadn't been up there among the clouds and back fifteen years I would surely have turned for home before now. But since we were almost there, Jesse might as well skate, and I might as well do the grocery shopping as planned, then join him. The music was gay and a combined smell of hot dogs, popcorn and wet wool greeted us. I left Jesse putting on his skates.

The blizzard kept getting worse, so I cut my list short and went back to the rink, and then became so enamored watching our grandson gracefully swoop over the ice that another hour slid by. When we finally did head for home I began to wonder seriously if we would ever get there. I thought even more nostalgically of our warm house, and how good a nice hot bath would feel that night, and a quiet evening by the fire. Even more cars were abandoned and I felt as if I were steering a boat the way our own rear end was swaying from side to side. Would that we had some of that fertilizer for ballast about now! I crept, reasoning that if you go slow enough when you bump into something, it isn't a very hard bump. Fortunately all the uphills had been on the way going, now the road was level or downhill.

The snow had turned fine and sifting, the kind that forms great drifts, and can blow on for hours and hours, and even days in Connecticut. It was coming sort of sideways, finding the tiniest cracks around the car windows. It felt like little pricks of ice on our faces.

Surely our guardian angels were working overtime to get us back home that day. It should have taken a half hour and it took two hours! Nothing ever looked quite as good to me as our house. We drove the car in the garage and headed through the laundry towards the kitchen with armfuls of groceries. Jesse walked on ahead to turn on the lights. I'd left the washing machine going and now it would be full of nice clean clothes ready for the dryer. What a blessing, I thought, are all these modern utilities that simplify life so much and make us impervious to weather.

In the dim light and balancing bundles I opened the door of the washing machine to shift our nice clean clothes to the dryer. With no warning I was nearly swept off my feet by a deluge of hot water which poured out the front opening and all over me, bringing with it yards and yards of steaming sheets and hot suds. In the shock of the moment I dropped everything. Surely, I thought dizzily, it must soon be empty of water and stop, but no. Something in the innermost workings was obviously amiss because the water kept boiling out while I kept trying to stuff the sheets back, so I could close the door. By now we were afloat in both kitchen and laundry. Oranges, apples, and potatoes all cheerfully bobbed about in the soapy suds amongst odd bits of paper bags, newly washed clothes, and bath towels. With Jesse and me standing ankle deep, and while hot water was pouring down inside our shoes, we both pushed against the water force until we finally got the machine door closed. Now at least the flow of new water stopped. But we must cope with what seethed around us, and quickly, to get the small flood out before it rose up over the step to the living room and did real damage. Seizing buckets and brooms we scooped and swept like mad. This hadn't been exactly the kind of hot bath I'd been anticipating!

"They never tell you about this in the washing machine ads," I exclaimed breathlessly to Jesse as we both worked feverishly, swishing water through the back door into the snowy night.

Outdoors the air was still blowing with fine flakes and it was so freezing cold that the water we swept rapidly froze into a solid sheet of ice on the door sill and beyond. Icicles cracking off the eaves added an ominous clinking.

After about an hour we had ourselves reasonably mopped

and dried and decided it was time to get dinner. I turned on the spigot at the sink and found there was no water. There was just no water anywhere in the house. The well and pump had given their all. First a deluge and then a drought. And here we had been nonchalantly sweeping the last water in our lives out the door.

Luckily we live on a brook. Presently we were slipping down the snowy bank, each with a pail, and cracking ice in the stream down under lots of inches of snow. It is amazing how little water you can get along with when you really have to. By the time Bob got home, and his drive also was a slow one, we had dinner simmering and had evolved a system of dry-cleaning the utensils with paper towels before a brief swish through a small bowl of treasured water. As a special luxury we each had a half a cup saved out to brush our teeth with that night.

A couple of hours later, as I said goodnight to Jesse who was tucked under the covers, he looked up and said, "Grandma, would you have time to tell me about another adventure you had, maybe about Indians or something—Guatemala Indians would be all right."

In a few days Jesse is gone. We move out of the realm of $pi\text{-}R^2$ and ^{3}, of spheres and cube roots, of blizzards and blue ice. The attic is folded back into its slumbering past, the water supply has quieted down. The house is singularly quiet. There remains only a rubber band slingshot caught in the branches of the jade tree.

3

March is restless and wild and windswept

MARCH WINDS TOSS KITES high up into a blue sky where white clouds are racing. March is the month of melting snow running in streams along the gutters beside the road, and small boys with cold red hands building dams and waterfalls after school.

March is a pair of mallards returning to our brook to raise their annual family. The voice of the ducks echoes over the meadow before dawn, and by day the pair wheels across the sky, the lady always a length or two behind her mate. Redwing blackbirds commune in the swamps while five bright blue jays perch in the maple facing the morning sun, puffing up their soft gray breast feathers. The cardinal's song has a hauntingly sweet quality, and a gay little brown sparrow somewhat hesitatingly chants his melody.

The March sun is a warming one, and turns the wet oak leaves to a rusty gold. The light is different. A rich glow in the air on certain days hints of what lies ahead. The sun is not hot yet, the temperature drops below freezing at night, and morning frost whitens the meadow. But you feel a difference in the air and find joy in it.

This is the month of sudden changes. One day the beginnings of spring are in the air, the next white flakes are flying. How many times the "last snow" falls or is it the first spring shower that happens to come down in flakes? A March snow serves a special purpose. Against its whiteness a rainbow of crocuses fairly preen themselves in sweeps and drifts along the gray stone walls.

In March winter is holding back and spring is pulling forward. Something holds and something pulls inside of us too. We are caught between two forces and sometimes nearly torn asunder. In the days of ghosts and witches, I'm sure that March was their season of special revels!

A restlessness in our bones responds to the wild restless winds of the month. The wind in January wakens a kind of strength. February storms rouse our spirits and hearten our defenses. But a tearing March wind howls through us exposing lonely and unfamiliar areas.

We are not at home with the strange impulses and wild, undisciplined thoughts that go blowing through our minds and emotions. Some days confidence shrinks to the size of a pea, and the backbone feels like a feather. We want to be somewhere else, and don't know where—want to be someone else and don't know who.

This is the time of year we long to be loved and told we are wonderful. Therefore it is a good moment to begin loving and appreciating others *and telling them about it.* It has been said that in a sense, we provide the love with which we are loved. Constructive and outgoing emotions open up certain channels of feeling. An inflowing love and understanding reaches through to us along these same channels.

What is March? It is change—in nature it is the change from winter to spring. We human beings tend to cling, even as winter does. The young are tempted and drawn to the new and untried, older people hesitate with the unknown. Whatever our age we are partly young and partly old. We think we welcome change. Sometimes we do and it brings wonderful new eras and experiences, broad horizons and excitement generally. But change does not always come smoothly and rhythmically. Occasionally it tosses us about uncomfortably.

Other strange needs of the month may invade private and inner corners that we had forgotten we had. Wistful parts of us, usually snugged out of sight by people, and gay interesting activities, suddenly stand bare, exposed, and raw—and worries come. How did that particular anxiety get back? I thought I had disposed of that one years ago, surely it has no power over me now! Where did this thought come from? Who is this stranger, you wonder in desperation when you can't sleep some night and wander around the house feeling sorry for yourself.

"Oh, come," I say to myself impatiently and with a great effort turn my thinking into a positive vein.

There is the day I find myself submerged in negative thoughts and wishing someone else would solve things for me. Emerson has a lot to say about this in his Essay on Self-Reliance. One especially meaningful passage is, "A man should learn to detect and watch that gleam of light which flashes across his mind from within more than the lustre of the firmament of bards and sages. Yet he dismisses without notice his thought because it is his."

Of course sometimes you can't find your gleam of light or turn your thoughts in any direction. They have you enthralled and turn you their way. When one of these moods descends, if you can just hold on and go about your business and not make any important decisions or outward changes, these times pass too. They pass as certainly as a stormy March day merges into a sunny, warm, spring one. It is your faith that helps you weather these times. And exactly what it faith? "Faith is the bird that feels the light and sings when the dawn is still dark," Rabindranath Tagore says. "Faith is the lack of resistance to that which you hope to receive," says Ambrose Worrall. It is interesting to make up your own definitions of faith and find the one that is particularly right for you.

Fortunately life itself keeps us level if we will let it. There are always blankets to bind, plants to water, rugs to hook, curtains to wash, meals to get, the weekly shopping. We are always needed in various places by friends and family. As we tuck ourselves and our restlessness aside for the day, and proceed with the business of living, the things in our outer and visible world give us a boost out of any kind of inward slough. It is best if we can balance reaction with action, emotion with motion. If we take action constructively and move forward in any direction, even without enthusiasm, something automatically happens to lift and change a gloomy state of mind. It alters as our direction develops purpose. I cheer myself too by remembering that a time of confusion and uncertainty often comes before a period of clarity and strength.

This is the March of it. The wind that blows in such restlessness, loose-end feelings, yearnings and confusions, also, in due time, blows them out. It has to because it is time to clear the woods of brush and dead branches, to prune the roses, and get on with spring.

Today was a wonderful day beginning with creamed eggs on toast for breakfast. We could hardly wait to get outdoors since the sun shone warm and there was no wind. I began raking the stones off the grass where the snowplow had pushed them. Bob in his shop was sanding the wooden counter top from the kitchen that had become rather marked up. Bob Jr. and Susan's visit in May inspires us to many small repairs around the place, indoors and out. My husband's next project was to prune the grapes. In summer great fifteen-foot runners take a firm grip on the roof shingles and threaten to pull the house apart. Each year they must be disciplined. I took last fall's homemade grape juice out of the freezer. It seemed appropriate to drink it on the morning of the pruning.

I know it is March some week-end morning when I see my husband down in the meadow in rubber boots putting the south fork of the brook back in its bed. Every winter this stream runs over its bank and converts the south meadow into a bog. In June wild iris thrives here and golden meadow parsnips. Water hemlock, Canada lilies, and all sorts of semi-boggy plants flourish as a result of the vagaries of this stream.

However, the brook has a perfectly good bed and should obviously be in it, or at least should be guided back to it once a year. Bob clears out old leaves and extra silt that slows the flow and builds up the bank into a sort of dike and soon the water is back where it belongs. One year he had to cut a huge, thick root, more than a foot in diameter, that was blocking the stream. The tree, a fifty-foot dying elm, subsequently did die and then became a true treasure. The bark completely peeled off and the limbs, stark and naked, turned a most beautiful silver gray which they still are today. Almost all the branches are intact and the lovely elm shape is prominent throughout the year.

Against the lush greenness of summer, this delicate tracery of gray stands out clearly. In winter the silvery trunk and branches are a contrast to the dark evergreens beyond. The dead elm is where it could do no harm should a storm blow it down. We enjoy the look of an occasional gray tree among the lush green ones, and always let a few dead ones stand on the place. We especially like this elm and so do woodpeckers who nest there every year.

After solving the wayward brook, Bob moves over to prune the other brook that flows along our land to the west. This one stays in its bed all year, but bordering branches trail down in the water and catch floating leaves and slow the stream. On the banks interesting old logs are hidden by brush and small whip-like saplings. Working together we remove clutter everywhere. We clear around a hemlock so it can grow freely, pull a tangle of vines off a witch hazel tree, free a spice bush, and trim back wild grapes from a black alder. We keep a path open along the brookside, and each year about this time "sculp" it into attractive vistas. Every bend presents a delightful view of water, mossy banks, old stumps, tumbled rocks and the deep sandy parts of the stream, the cool pools where trout retreat on warm summer days. Moving along slowly we take out what has grown to hamper the views. I pile fallen branches and prunings in a great heap for a bonfire next month when Jeff comes down, and all the while I am tasting the sweet potatoes wrapped in silver paper we will bake in the coals for that first picnic of the season.

Near the water we came across two empty birds' nests, not more than four feet from the ground. They were made of coarse sticks and belonged to the redwing blackbirds that we hear every day now. The nests were cleverly concealed and could never have been found when surrounding branches and vines were in leaf. From far up the stream we heard the distant voice of the mallards who were perhaps considering various nesting sites. In the swampy places skunk cabbage was sending up from the muck fabulous shell-like shapes, each one different in form and color. The sun shone on the tan meadow grass and on the boughs of the apple trees with a whiteness and a fresh-washed look.

March teaches us to be adaptable.
Lilja Rogers writes:

> First a howling blizzard woke us
> Then the rain came down to soak us,
> And now before the eye can focus—
> Crocus.

There is a wonderful way to develop the ability to adapt—and not only to weather but to all changes. It is a simple drill with a far-reaching effect. Do something new and different once each day for a while, and not necessarily anything extremely unusual or startlingly new. It can be merely doing a familiar thing in a different way. If you usually go out the front door, leave by the side door one morning instead. If you always put on your left shoe first, try putting on the right one, or walk down a different side of the street from the one you are used to.

This, a psychologist friend recently told us, forms new pathways in the brain. When you next meet a block in some direction of thinking or action, you will be able to accept it constructively and come up with a way around the situation which previously might have seemed a dead end.

He likened this doing something new and different every day to playing scales on the piano. Scales gradually develop in your fingers the agility to play the Moonlight Sonata. The adaptability exercise trains into the part of your brain that must adjust to new directions a flexibility, and a receptivity to the unexpected.

Until I tried this I always thought I was the world's most adaptable person. To my amazement, I held on quite firmly in some areas and resisted change. You may discover the same thing about yourself.

Bob went into St. Patrick's Cathedral in New York City one day by way of doing something different. He had never been in it before although he had passed it many times. It provided a pleasant and welcome break, a few moments of complete peace in beautiful quiet surroundings, while beyond the thick walls the city hummed and hurried. We've both discovered all sorts of places, stores, roads, books that we never knew existed as we've done the simple exercise. Entirely apart from developing the ability to adapt, this discipline is also rewarding and pleasant in the doing, and in the new doors it opens.

Mrs. Glover taught me how to make the easiest and most ambrosial gingerbread, and no mix involved. I had taken her for a drive and we stopped at the Emporium for molasses, and that led to gingerbread. Her recipe dates back to her grandmother's grandmother and has its roots firmly in New England.

I came right home and made the gingerbread, which of course, led to whipped cream! We forgot calories and no harm done. Half the pleasure of baking gingerbread is the fragrance while it cooks. Mrs. Glover's recipe is ¾ cup of molasses, ½ cup boiling water, ¾ cup sugar, 1 egg, ½ cup melted butter or margarine. Melt and blend everything together over low heat except the egg. Stir constantly. Take off the stove and add the egg, ¾ teaspoon cinnamon, ½ teaspoon cloves, ½ teaspoon nutmeg, 1 level teaspoon soda, 1½ cups sifted white flour. Mix well. Bake in 8 x 8, 2 inch deep, greased pan in a 350° oven for about thirty minutes. Presently the whole house smells of gingerbread.

I love to cook. I'm not a complicated or gourmet cook. I don't spend hours and hours in the kitchen composing intricate sauces and casseroles. I greatly enjoy preparing meals—simple ones. It is the process I like—the textures, the fragrances, the creativity involved. The surprises of all kinds that result and the constant experiments and new discoveries are a joy.

My evolution as a cook began when we first moved to Connecticut. I don't know what this attractive rolling green countryside has to do with it. Maybe it is partly our kitchen with the view one way into the greenhouse and the other direction into the north meadow.

When I was small I used to sit in the basement kitchen of our house in Spuyten Duyvil where I was born and watch Delia cook on the old-fashioned wood stove. I can't ever remember that Delia had a day off because we lived way out in the country and the only way you got places was by horse and buggy. Nor can I remember that this concerned her. The lives, interests, pleasures and problems of our family were hers. She was part of us—a vital part, and she loved to cook. She always used large kettles, wooden spoons, and had a casual way of pouring flour or any ingredients into things without ever measuring. Perhaps by osmosis I absorbed more than I knew in those early days. Anyhow, all the while she mixed up delectable cookies and pies, pancakes and biscuits light as air, she spun wonderful yarns about the wee folk in Ireland. I enjoyed fairy tales in all forms and here I had them alive.

My kitchen memories after Bob and I were married also involved someone else doing the cooking. When our three children were small we had Mary from Trinidad who settled in for years and made, beside the usual meals, blueberry ice cream which I will never forget and fabulous chocolate soufflé. Her soufflé rose to the oven roof and came to the table with a slight crack across the top, inside of which you could watch the chocolate still souffling. It was not until the children grew up and left home that I became the cook. I remember telling a friend that I didn't much like to prepare meals and that this was going to be difficult and would she please tell me some quick and easy recipes so I could spend a minimum of time in the kitchen. This she obligingly did and commented sort of sadly that if I didn't like to cook I was missing a lot. How right she turned out to be, but it took me several years to find this out.

I was a terrible cook when I began, and Bob was extremely good-natured and long-suffering. Then I learned to make bread. If I was in a wonderful mood it seemed to rise higher. Everything came out better if I cooked in a leisurely manner and enjoyed myself. The pleasure of preparing meals crept up on me slowly. I began to think about food as being sustenance, not just the ingredients of a meal because it's dinner time.

The next step was the revelation of how good foods feel as you prepare them. Crisp vegetables, fresh from the garden, were so great to handle. I like to get into a pie with both hands. I enjoy getting my hands into the act of whatever I am making. You encounter such a pleasing variety of textures in fruits, vegetables, pies and cakes, and, of course, meats. It gives you a good solid feel to handle a thick steak or leg of lamb and to know that what you are preparing will nourish, revitalize and energize those you love.

Another of the delights of cooking are the smells involved. Everything smells so good in process and so do the raw ingredients. How fresh the fragrance of cottage cheese when you first open the carton, or of parsley when you chop it up, and of apples as you pare them for sauce or pie. Cooking is a woman's natural world, I guess, and I am delighted to have discovered this world and to find it a compatible one. I now feel for those who don't like to cook just as my friend some years back thought that I was missing something vital. Certain women rely regularly on TV dinners or something quick out of the freezer. At times we all need the freezer and quick-heated leftovers, on days when life crowds in on us. But in the main, if we can plan time to cook without pressure or rush, great joy and satisfaction lie in all aspects of it.

Surely it is possible that you impart something to the food you handle and work with, and that what you impart depends on your mood. It has been proven that tender loving care affects plants and children, why not food? These days we are told that negative thinking and depressed moods have a special slow vibration, that positive and joyous thinking has a quicker and different vibration. These vibrations can actually be photographed. Isn't it reasonable that such vibrations emanating from us affect whatever we are doing, including the food we prepare? Certainly from a practical angle, if you love what you are doing, you naturally pay attention, put your heart in it, and good results come.

Part of my satisfaction in cooking involves using certain natural foods. Raw, dark brown sugar is so amusing the way it appears to creep and crawl for a moment inside the sugar bowl after you disturb it. Sea salt is not only full of all sorts of beneficial minerals but has a wonderful tang and is quite different from ordinary salt. It is coarser and sparkles.

I enjoy utensils, too. I smile every time I behead an egg with some "scissors" made for the purpose. My little garlic press is great fun to use and so is a French whisk for scrambled eggs. The good old-fashioned wooden potato masher is another treasure. Did you ever try to buy one of these in a modern hardware store? You can purchase all kinds of potato mashers made of metal in a number of efficient shapes. But just a simple, good, old fashioned, wooden potato masher has gone the way of the woven clothes basket. Fortunately sometimes country stores stock these two favorite household items.

I am well aware that in life something for nothing is not the proper approach at all, but in cooking I often lean in this direction. By this I mean something heavenly in the way of a result with but little time spent making it. One, One, One Cookies are a fine example. One egg white, one cup of nuts, one cup of brown sugar, one teaspoon of vanilla. Into the beaten egg white beat the sugar, and add the nuts and vanilla. This all takes about five minutes. Bake in 200° oven for one hour. These meringue cookies are light as a breeze, simply heavenly, and how could they be quicker or easier?

More power to those of you who spend two or three days cooking for a party. Many is the meal of this nature that we have appreciated at someone else's home, and many is the chicken we've eaten, marinated for hours or days in this or that. But Fricassee Chicken purely boiled and thickened and served with its own gravy takes but little time and is also delicious. Actually I prefer chicken as chicken. This is how Bob feels about eggs. I'm forever adding to scrambled eggs such things as yogurt, powdered milk, chopped parsley, cut up liver, and, in season, rose petals. Bob is apt to say wistfully, "You know, I just like eggs."

It was a fresh, sunny day when I set forth in a gay mood for a town about an hour's drive away where I was to give a talk on Carefree Gardening. Since my book by that name came out, I am often asked to give lectures at garden clubs. I had a brand new wisp of a flower hat for the occasion. The roads were clear, the day brilliant, and my spirits high. I enjoy sharing our experiences here in the garden with others interested in growing things. It is fun to meet and exchange ideas with gardeners from different areas.

There is always a luncheon beforehand and someone is sure to say, "Now really, this carefree gardening you're going to speak about, I just don't believe it. There is no such thing. Gardening is plain hard work. Believe me, I know."

This pleases me and provides a real challenge. We have developed a relaxed, carefree kind of gardening, and a little skepticism ahead of time perfectly sets the stage for what I have to say. To the surprise of most people our methods and procedures do mean practically no upkeep. For us, gardening *is* carefree.

Of course I suppress my gloat when those incredulous souls come up after the lecture with a "Well, maybe," or even better, "Well, I'll have to admit, you've convinced me and now I can't wait to get home and try it."

The luncheon ahead always provides an opportunity to become acquainted with those I will be speaking to. During the shrimp and salad, I have altered many a talk as a result of what I have heard. Little did I think how I would change this one with the first spoonful of consomme.

I happily approached the town, which I will call Fairview, with my notes on Carefree Gardening tucked snugly in my purse. I was planning to use the notes as little as possible and was rehearsing my beginning as the car coasted through the clean, windswept March countryside.

I was contentedly sipping the delicious red consomme when the woman on my right turned to me and said,

"I've come all the way from western Pennsylvania to hear your talk on wild flowers—and I can't wait."

I nearly choked on the consomme.

"Oh, yes," said the woman across the table, "we're all so interested in wild flowers, we have a wonderful preserve here —you'll have to return next month and see it."

"Wild flowers," I heard myself say, as from a great distance. "Oh yes, we love them too." My voice, totally disconnected from me, seemed to run on and on inanely.

I had a talk on wild flowers but hadn't given it in years. This one had been on my calendar as Carefree Gardening. There were about six lectures in this month and next and they were all Carefree Gardening, I was sure. 'Somebody is crazy,' I thought wildly, '—or could it be me? Surely they had asked for Carefree Gardening.' But in the next few minutes it became very clear from the conversation around me that the error was mine, and that it was wild flowers I was to speak on in one hour.

"Have you ever grown Lythrum salicaria?" asked my neighbor. "We had some Decodon verticillatus given us and they are doing quite well, too. And last year the lousewort was heavenly."

"Clammy Cuphea is such a delightful little flower," said my other neighbor, "do you know that one?"

Surely this was only a nightmare. Any moment now I would wake up in my cozy bed at home far from Clammy Cuphea and Decodon.

My mind was a disjointed swirl of confusion while I ate I know not what. There was no use telling them of my error because then there would be not only me in a state of panic, but others as well. And this would never do.

When we finished lunch there remained one half hour before the lecture.

"I wonder if I could go out in the car alone and go over my notes." I asked my hostess. "Why certainly," she said cheerfully, "we have to set up some flower arrangements."

"Phew," I thought, collapsing into the car seat.

"Well, Jean," I said to myself briskly, "in just one half hour you are going to speak on wild flowers, so gather yourself together and start thinking." My middle was not merely butterflies, but flocks and flocks of swallows. My hands were like ice, and my head like a furnace.

"Nuts," said a voice inside, "don't take yourself so seriously. The world will continue about the same no matter what you say. Just review what you know about wild flowers, pray a little, and do the best you can. You've always dreamed that some day you'd be confident enough to lecture without notes. Here is your chance."

"We're all ready," said my hostess in what seemed two minutes. Off I started as if to one of these 14th century executions we had been reading about.

We had moved to Connecticut about fifteen years ago to a meadow, a brook, and a wood, where hundreds of wild flowers grew. We had added a number more and I had written an article or two on the subject. There was, however, rather a gap between these facts and an organized talk.

"And now I wish to present Mrs. Hersey, who will speak to us about wild flowers."

It was a good thing there was a table in front of me to conceal my shaking knees. I have learned if my hands feel shaky to hold them behind my back.

I began with the story of the wild, golden trout lilies one sunny April day that had first brought us to our land, and I went on to our move and the discovery of almost one hundred different sorts of flowers already thriving there. We had coaxed the newly added ones to grow successfully by matching the location where they grew wild with the one on our place where we set them out. I have little memory of what I said in detail. I happen to love every inch of our land, and on this wild and windy March day it was pleasant to recreate for the group before me spring, summer, and fall in our meadow, and to bring them word pictures of the stream with marsh marigolds, the woods starred with hepaticas, and the fields gold with sweeps of hawkweed.

My knees gradually steadied, my hands stopped shaking.

and I began having fun. The meadow, the brook, and our woods had come to my aid as they had many times before under quite other circumstances. The flowers had risen to the occasion, the wood betony, the water hemlock, the joe-pye-weed, and the purple asters. Names I had forgotten pricked my attention and they were included.

The response was warm and cordial and I headed home aching in every bone but in a sort of pleasant glow.

The first thing I did when I got into the house was to look up my correspondence. Sure enough, in the letter I had received nearly a year before and in my response, there in plain print, it said Wild Flowers.

The first thing I did next morning was to go to Klein's and buy a little wooden box filing system of cards. Now each lecture ahead has its own card with subject, place, hour, etc., and the date.

I never tire of the challenge of speaking to different groups. But I must say, I prefer to know what my subject is ahead of time. In the beginning there I stand and there sits the audience, and between us lies a chasm. I sense in those before me a state of mind cordial, but somewhat as follows: "Who is this woman and what has she to say—I hope Mary remembered the silver teapot, and that I made enough sandwiches, and I hope she doesn't talk too long because I have to meet Susan at dancing class." It is something like this that I begin to speak *at*. After a few minutes things happen, the chasm shrinks, the audience is no longer "a group" but a number of separate individuals. An indefinable something passes between us and for forty minutes or so we are linked by the subject and together we explore the new paths to which it leads. Being one with thirty women in a group in a home living room, or three hundred in an auditorium can be a most rewarding experience.

I was congratulating myself on making it through the winter without a cold. Right and left friends seemed to be taking to bed with a virus; I was keeping my fingers crossed. No problems for Bob and me so far.

Then one fine day I woke and couldn't swallow. There I lay full of aches and pains, and a cough—the works. I had no desire to move. I suppose if you are going to have a cold you might as well be thorough about it. Our doctor says the flu or a cold is a rather wonderful mechanism of nature, a warning, telling you to slow up and rest. It comes to stop you in your tracks when you need stopping. If you relax and rest, you can be preventing a heart attack, or something a lot worse. When you have a cold, he says go to bed and thank nature for sending the message. I guess life first nudges, then pushes, and in all ways tries to get us to realize our needs, and then, if necessary, knocks us down to tell us. Anyhow I lay there quite flat, sneezing, coughing, aching, while my husband most kindly and thoughtfully cooked. I was so sleepy that I slept most of the day with the cheerful feeling that my dripping nose and coughs were getting rid of a lot of poisons that needed to be disposed of.

A number of obligations lay ahead and I was vaguely trying to sort the ones I could eliminate when I realized I would have to eliminate them all. Then I felt free and even more relaxed. At first, I had the sensation of being put through a washing machine and wrung out thoroughly. I knew I had to give up, let go, and completely relinquish. When I was gradually able to do this, I felt an inner vitality stir. After a few more days I emerged from bed into the last stages of feeling rather like a limp, wet sheet hung on the line in the healing sun to dry, but a sheet blown by every breeze. It was a hazy but pleasant way to be. In another few days I was quite myself and rather the better for a rest.

There are many kinds of joy. There is one special variety that comes when you are creatively engaged in some project and using the part of you that is uniquely you. With each of us the job may vary, and greatly, but it will be one that is vitally important to you. At such a moment, in the doing, you feel *more than you are*. For the time you *are* more than you are. Thoughts greater than you know come. You are doing, saying, writing, organizing, producing, or perhaps just carrying on the day's activities but all in a brand new way and with an extra unplanned flourish. This is something you consciously have nothing to do with. It just happens. Nor can you make it happen. But you can provide the climate in which it is most likely to occur—a climate partly of openness, of expectancy, and a readiness to receive. It is the happening, the occurring that brings a special satisfaction like nothing else I know or have experienced. I don't say that it is necessarily vital to be a part of this sort of creative experience, but I do say that it is unique and rich. He who has known these golden moments of relatedness to something greater than he, and far beyond, while engaged in a project at hand, is lucky indeed and will at once recognize what I am talking about.

One day I was strolling through Food Fair with my mind on potatoes when out of the tail of my eye I caught a glimpse of rose bushes. These I could resist because our rose bed is full. We have eighteen roses, and when we get a new one we have to part with an old one because eighteen is exactly the number we want to have and take care of. But next to the roses was a package of raspberries—five plants for $1.69. The canes were about two feet high. It was the first day of spring officially even if nature hadn't acquiesced. The temperature outside was 30° and a cold wind was blowing. The bright red raspberries on the package made my mouth water. The lush, scarlet fruit, huge and realistic, transported me to next July. I could smell those ripe berries, feel them, and taste them gathered with the morning dew on them. I could imagine the flavor when they were eaten with sugar and cream for breakfast on the terrace, with the scent of roses all around.

Of course we had pulled out a lot of raspberries that had taken over the vegetable garden about two years ago, and given them up. The ground was frozen solid at the moment so how could I plant them. But these inner voices were silenced by irresistible tiny green shoots barely visible here and there along the canes. One of the men was placing chlorox bottles in rows on a shelf. He was singing in a rich baritone, "My heart belongs to all of you," as we women with our wire baskets gradually moved along the aisles. Listening to this cheery music I picked up the raspberries which were obviously ours.

You always meet your friends in Food Fair. Bessie and Bill had just returned from the South—hadn't even been home yet. They had a look of holiday about them—sort of free and suntanned. We talked several moments and then down another aisle I conversed a bit longer with two other friends. With someone I didn't even know I was soon discussing whether the oranges were sweet or sour. Cold though it was, there was a lilt in the air and in my spirits. A little of Bessie and Bill's holiday mood had rubbed off on me. "My heart belongs to all of you" echoed through the store and followed me out to the car with the raspberries. I would now go looking for kite string.

Fishermen have a faraway look in their eyes, the same kind of look that gardeners have. Fishermen dream of next season as we gardeners do—of next season's fish bigger and better, as I envision next season's roses larger and lovelier. It turned out to be a fishing tackle shop that seemed likely to provide the rather rare string that our aristocratic Christmas kite demanded. In the search I had explored all local hardware stores and sporting goods stores and the rough and rugged wharves of Norwalk. I made quite a few new acquaintances but had not been able to locate five hundred yards of single filament nylon that tested to 50 pounds. I had even been referred to a prominent kite flier in the vicinity who cordially led me far afield on the phone and into all sorts of kite lore, but had no convictions about where to get our five hundred yards. I had been assured by a fishing tackle shop in Norwalk that they had the very thing, but when I got there it turned out to be in one-hundred yard pieces and you can't tie knots in kite string. Finally another fishing tackle shop on this, the first day of spring, said they would have a special order made up for us. Before it even got off the ground this kite was leading us a merry chase!

When you plant early, you bring spring early. We always like to get peas, spinach, lettuce, parsley, beets and carrots in this month. We stand on chilly ground with slightly frosted fingers and drop seeds in the long rows of rich brown earth. We begin to eat our spinach in May and our lettuce too when most people are merely thinking about planting. Our seeds have arrived, and we keep looking at them and feeling them through the packages. Here in a small corrugated box that you can readily lift with one hand lies a whole summer garden with hundreds of pounds of all kinds of crops and part of next winter's produce too. There is still a couple of inches of frost on top of the vegetable garden. Each morning Bob goes out with a fork to test it, but it is hard and frozen.

Mr. Messex who works in Hartman's Hardware lives near us and said he would rototill the area. He is waiting to dig his own garden too. Each week when I go into the shop we compare notes on how solid with frost our respective gardens are.

"I won't dig yours before ours," he says, "or your peas will come up and you'll win the race."

We have a friendly rivalry about who will eat the first peas. Last year we had an unfair advantage because the woodchucks beheaded all of his. So this year competition is keen.

At long last the day comes—the fork goes down in the ground everywhere. We woke to a brilliant sunny morning and about ten o'clock heard Mr. Messex arrive with his rototiller. With great pleasure Bob and I stood by and watched the rich earth fold in on itself as his tiller wove back and forth over the dark ground. The remnants of hay and leaves—last summer's mulch—and fertilizer scattered last month were all stirred in. Bob raked the area smooth, and with string and rule measured out the rows. Never a peeper peeped while we planted onions, peas, radishes, carrots and beets. Since the moon was waning we got in the root crops and this is right. According to Mrs. Glover's country lore which we follow, the peas which are an above-ground crop should go in during a waxing moon. However, we couldn't wait any longer since we like to get peas planted as near St. Patrick's Day as possible and we were late. A new moon will rise in a few days so we'll do lettuce, spinach and parsley then.

March is going out like a lion this year. A howling wind all but blows my hair off as it whips through gray days of rain, snow, sleet and temperatures in the 20's and teens. What of our seeds planted a few days ago? In discouragement perhaps they will go down where it *may* be warmer rather than up into this.

Since Nick is coming on April 1st to rebuild the greenhouse we have had to move all the orchids into the shop and the house. As soon as we did this the temperature plummetted. Bob goes out in the middle of the night to adjust lamps to keep the orchids warm. Living intimately with orchids seems like a subject we'll be qualified to expand on at spring dinner parties. I wash dishes around Lycaste Skinneri, the White Nun orchid. Now in bud, this one likes the dishwater steam and hourly the buds expand, but it is rather a hazard balancing the dripping pots on the counter on all sides of the plant. Equally complex is the process of doing the washing when the tops of both washer and dryer are covered with flowering orchids. Dendrobiums and great white Cattleyas stand among the fresh, dry sheets, and they all bounce a little as the towels and shirts spin in the cycle. The combination of glamourous orchids and nearby earthy potatoes, onions, and oranges creates a rather bizarre atmosphere in our otherwise conventional blue laundry.

Here we are with spring officially more than a week old

and the peepers still don't know a thing about it, and even the birds have stopped singing, and birds are usually incorrigible optimists.

On the last day of the month I drew close to Mrs. Glover's stove and watched her hook her rug while fine flakes drifted down outside the window.

"Do you think spring will ever come?" I asked.

Mrs. Glover looked out at the snow thoughtfully, and, drawing a piece of yarn through the burlap with her hook, replied succinctly,

"Always has."

PART 2

Season of flowers, of deep involvement

OUR CEILING THESE DAYS is high as the heavens, our walls stretch to the horizon. With all our senses alert we have merged with the world of nature. We become keenly aware of the sounds, the smells, the feel of everything, and gradually find ourselves an integral part of it all.

Growth begins slowly at first but gathers momentum. Soon we are knee-deep in blossoms—daffodils, golden hawkweed, daisies—all streaming through the fields. Great Oriental poppies open over night. Each blade of meadow grass seems to crowd its neighbor blade for room to stand. Action and reaction are so fast you must be alert to keep track. The seeds you plant one day in an earth moist and fresh after a spring shower are up three days later. We not only sense the rush of productivity on all sides but we smell it. The warming soil, the meadow, the woods, and even the stream, each has its special scent. And as you walk abroad a fragrance you do not know wafts over a hedge.

Part of the excitement is our participation. We plant, we fertilize, we mulch, we cultivate, we cope with insects. We are involved and care about each new unfolding, each new flower and leafing tree. In every part of the garden something calls, needs must be met. Within us a new strength stirs, quickens, and moves out to meet and be a vital part of a burgeoning world.

As we let go and merge with this season of flowers and rampant growth, we become aware of the light touch of a force that surrounds us, a force much greater than we.

4

April is a kind of unfolding

APRIL IS LIKE THE RAGGEDY, wandering gypsy lad of the fairy tale. When he moves streaks of gold show beneath his torn garments and you suspect that this elfin creature is actually a prince in disguise. April is just that. There are raggedy, cold days, dark black ones, but all through the month for a second, for an hour, or for three days at a stretch you glimpse pure gold. The weeks pass and the rags slip away, a shred at a time. Toward the end of the month his royal highness stands before you.

We seem to shed winter the way the gypsy sheds his rags—a little at a time. We welcome the breeze that blows with spring warmth over bare arms and through the hair. The sunny ground feels good to touch again. Spring stirs and wakens in both spirit and landscape.

Gardens grow almost visibly in the showers of the month. The rain, so gentle, turns off and on like a faucet, and between showers sharp slivers of sunlight streak through the blue-gray clouds. A pink haze lies over the bare-branched trees down by the brook. Hemlocks are a yellow-green, our willow a streaming gold, and a pair of emerald dragonflies hovers over the still pool below the terrace. While I watch the grass grows greener, and out every window is an invitation I cannot resist.

Around the neighborhood small bright-colored tents spring up in front yards, and lawns are dusted white with plant food. Every day at dusk the first Carolina wren sings his enchanting song from the topmost branch of a stark dead tree standing along the north wall. One night I am getting dinner, stirring a pot of stew with one hand while pruning the Matterhorn with the other. This newly arrived All American Rose Selection rose is in the kitchen sink "plumping up." What a beautiful sturdy plant, and how it will enhance the rose bed.

Mingled with all of April's delights comes our annual feud with the barn swallows. These handsome, graceful, swooping birds are determined to nest in the garage right above the car. Every morning when Bob first opens the door the birds are in and up on the beams cooing and deciding where to build. Equally determined, Bob, flourishing a bamboo leaf rake, chases them out. While one circles out the other circles in. It is rather like trying to get a firm hold on a stream of water. The first second both swallows are out, I, who have been refereeing the battle, pull down the door with a wham. They soar off over the treetops in great and lovely scallops.

It is romantic, no doubt, to have swallows nesting in the barn, but the practical in us rises above the romantic. The year the phoebes built on top of the shiny metal light fixture outside the garage door we were charmed and went right along with them. It was astonishing how they secured their nest to the slippery chrome. We refrained from using that light until the last fledgling had flown off. Another time we sacrificed one of Bob's rubbers that he had inadvertently left heel up and toe down in the rose arbor. A pair of sparrows took it over. But swallows in the garage, no! The ways of nature are ever mysterious. That was the spring that the attractive new birdhouse was left uninhabited.

These nights we drift off to sleep to the sound of the peepers who have arrived at last in this late season. We wake to the friendly gobbling of the mallard ducks along the stream, the rain on the roof, and the slosh of the rain barrel spilling over.

This is the year we love rain, yes, everything about it. In a personal and private glow I walk about under my yellow umbrella that, when wet, turns gold as the willow branches.

Last week I bought a light plastic raincoat—a really waterproof one, not merely water repellant. I asked the saleswoman for a raincoat you could sit in a puddle with. I don't actually go about sitting in puddles, but I do like to know I can.

Spring showers are always appreciated. What a joy to hear the drops descend in a torrent that runs along the gutters of the house. Rain floods the red bricks of the terrace and brings out their tapestry colors. It pours into the rain barrel and flows over the rim to green the surrounding grass. The drive is a series of puddles, and a stream falls beside the front door from the wooden gutter overhead. We can almost feel the grateful earth soak it up as the sap rises in the trees, and buds everywhere begin to unfold.

Rain is particularly welcome this year because of the drought last summer and fall. There never was such a drought in the memory of Mrs. Glover whom I always consider to be the oldest inhabitant. For months the reservoirs fell lower and lower.

"Only 58 more days of water unless it rains," the radio ominously announced.

We all begin to save water, using as little as possible. Mr. Allen, the pump man from Bethel, said, "As long as your well doesn't cough and sputter you are all right. But if it shoots air, watch out!"

Then came the day. It coughed and sputtered *and* "shot air." We rationed a half a glass of water for teeth each night, and bathed by the inch instead of the tub-full. Our well is 176 feet deep and surely the water table is low if at that depth it was hesitating.

One sunny blue fall day followed another. We reveled in long hours on the beach sunning, and driving with the top down. This was California weather and we should be appreciative, everyone kept telling everyone else, as we all hopefully looked for a cloud on the horizon that might bring a downpour. But alas, the rare dark cloud that did appear floated away with never a drop of water in it.

Along the roadsides leaves hung limp. Our stream dried altogether in places for the first time in our fifteen years in Connecticut. Erstwhile thrifty ponds where ducks had played and swans glided turned to dried, baked mudholes. It was sad to watch the whole countryside parch and wither. The Saugatuck Reservoir, just the other side of Pop's Mountain, is a man-made one. One fine day the islands were no longer islands, and the outlying areas of the old town of Valley Forge emerged. On week-ends we would climb around these islands that had once been hilltops and explore where no man had tramped since the area had been flooded twenty-five years before. The mud-caked reservoir in places was hard and cracked like mosaic. You could see dried hollows where fish had hovered and spawned.

Buckley's Four Corners came into view first and here were the stone foundations of a great barn and Mr. Buckley's house across the way. We found the old well and one lone child's tin soldier. I could imagine Mr. Buckley sitting on his porch reading the Sears Catalogue and probably rocking in an old-fashioned wooden rocker as he smoked his pipe. Greenery from the great maple whose stump was still there must have shaded him from the summer sun, while across the way his cows grazed, flicked off flies with their tails, and chewed their cuds.

It was eerie to see roads, their tarred surfaces still intact, coming up out of the blue water, and equally eerie was a No Man's Land of silvery gray tree stumps whose tops had been cut off before the town was flooded.

Walking in that weird area of sun-baked desolation always gave me an uneasy feeling. I guess a ghost town has ghosts. It was a pleasant relief to return to our live and thriving valley. Dry as it was, our land was at least living. Here was a basic vitality and a going concern while Valley Forge was a very dead past.

It is fine to be able to delve briefly into the past. We learn much from what has gone before us, both in the world generally and in our personal lives. We ought always to be ready to look back, but never to stay back. It is easy to hold on too tightly to what was, to "the way things used to be," especially if some certain way was unusually good. Yet if we can loose the good and move on ahead a greater good often comes. We are tempted, all of us, to hold onto ideas also that have served their term and need updating. Walking around erstwhile Valley Forge always gave me an inward shake and a reminder to live in the now in both thought and action.

After last fall's drought no wonder we listen to this April rain with joy—let it drip, mizzle, pour, let rivers run anywhere they want to. The thirsty earth drinks up the water gratefully. And day by day, the reservoir rises. How long since we have heard the water pounding over the dam? It will be a great day when a wind blowing down the gorge brings that welcome sound. It is still not imminent.

One bright Sunday we were returning from a week-end in Rye. For the first time this year we put the top of our convertible down and the sun and air were pleasant. Pansies burgeoned in people's front gardens. Banks of forsythia showed touches of early gold. An indefinite number of young children seemed to appear on every side street. With small carts and wagons they coasted down tarred roads where slopes were gradual. An automobile passed with a trailer and a boat. Another car swung by with trees waving out the back window. At a nursery just off the road we caught sight of a dozen or so appealing, sturdy, balled dogwoods, obviously needing some place to grow. We paused and then, of course, were lost, and joined the spring parade with three trees rising up out of our back seat. Crowded at my feet were boxes of pansies. I never saw larger flowers, yellow, white, and a wonderful shade of inky blue. Each blossom was the size of my palm.

Back home we admired the new trees, each one about six feet tall and covered with buds. Larry, the teenager who often helps us, came over with a friend and two girls. The girls giggled in the car while he and his pal helped Bob plant the trees near the terrace. Bob was putting the shovel away when the rain descended, and it showered intermittently for a week.

If you could compress nature's year into a matter of seconds, it would be rather like a long, slow breath. The inbreath is fall, a building tension, a filling up. Winter comes when you've taken in all you can, all the richness of summer's end and autumn harvest, and when you hold a moment. This is a still period when the world is frozen and white and solid and all growth pauses. Within us we feel a corresponding pause, a waiting. Then comes spring, the turn of the tide, the slow breathing out, the letting go. Streams let go of their ice, snow melts in the sun to run rivers over the land. The spirit also seems to loose itself and move freely again. The long slim outbreath extends all through spring and summer. At summer's end comes another lull, a moment of hesitation as when the outgoing tide, dead low, pauses before the inflow. Then again the inbreath and the rhythm of the year repeats.

This alternating tension and relaxation are a part of daily living. How often we take a deep breath either literally or figuratively before we tackle a difficult job. The tension, the inbreath, is the preparation, the relaxation, the outbreath comes in the doing. Ideally we release the tension in the actions of the day and meet the evening free from any residue.

Within is the microcosm, the breath we draw. Without is the macrocosm, the long, slow, turning breath of a year. Now in April the year is letting go, and we feel ourselves let go with it and relax as a new season is born.

One morning I heard Bob back out of the garage to drive to work, but he presently reappeared. He put his head around the kitchen door and said three words—April Words—"Peas are up."

It had been raining all day yesterday and most of the day before, turning bare trees a purple black, and budding trees to dusty pink. In the ground all the seeds were swelling with promise. I had stirred the earth a little in the pea row, and found a few pale white sprouts attached to swollen seeds. Now I immediately went out in the light rain. Standing on the gravel drive beside a cluster of flowering johnny-jump-ups I could see tiny, green, beginning pea leaves flat on the ground all down the row. Yes, they are up. The first seeds planted and the first seeds to come. And not only the pea seeds are up. On closer look, the spinach, too, lay like a row of soft green feathers over the rich black earth. This last rain had done it, and the lettuce was like sprinkles of chartreuse salt over the same black earth. Twin radish leaves were unfolding. With imagination you could see a hint of carrot. The whole garden was stirring, everywhere outdoors something was happening, and above and over it all birds high in the branches were exchanging melodies.

In the meadow the first daffodils were opening. I picked them—six jonquils with great yellow trumpets for the dinner table that night. There is no scent like the first daffodils in the morning freshness. What a wonderful note to start the day on.

As more of our daffodils open each day we gather armfuls for our house and for friends. We keep a plastic pail half filled with water in the car. Wherever we go the next few weeks we carry blossoms with us. At home I arrange them in every room in the house including the bathrooms, and often in a clear glass vase so the crisscrossing pattern of their attractive green stems is visible.

Daffodils are the ancient Chinese symbol of good fortune. Surely they bring every kind of good fortune to those of us who dig them in each fall. If you have any problems or concerns, and who hasn't at times, take them out to where the sun shines on the daffodils and wander all through them. View them back lit, front lit, side lit. Smell them, feel them, touch the petals, the stems and leaves, and feel their alive crispness. Watch the breeze stir them. You'll know how Wordsworth felt.

And your problem of an hour ago? What was it anyhow? You may not even remember—or if you do, you may well have a new point of view about it. Something happens when you linger in a meadow with a thousand daffodils for minutes, or hours. Changes occur within you. Events fall into proper perspective. Even persistent anxieties shrink a little and fit into their true place in the scheme of things.

Dandelions are beautiful. Just pick one blossom, take a magnifying glass and study the pattern of the petals. There is no brighter gold than that of a dandelion in the sunshine. Once we were climbing through the Alpine meadows in Switzerland and were attracted by great streaks of gold higher up. Wondering what rare Swiss plant this could be, we climbed higher and higher. Of course they turned out to be our old friends. The intriguing French "Dent de Lion" is the source of our name for them.

There is real virtue in dandelions, and with a little different point of view they are no longer a menace, even when they grow in the lawn. What other flower blossoms in New England in December after three inches of snow and almost three months of intermittent frost? These are the first flowers of spring as well as the last of autumn. As an added bonus, the early leaves are delicious in salads.

Obviously nobody wants dandelions to take over the lawn, but we have evolved a delightful compromise, a sort of practical relationship with these bright gold flowers. We enjoy their spring bloom, and along in May drop a little weed killer in the center of each plant. A few seeds escape so we never are quite free of them. But this treatment limits their spread. We have flowers very early in the spring and almost up until Christmas, but they never get too out of hand. And perhaps what is most important, we simply do not worry about them.

The magic round seed globe of the dandelion is as attractive as the flower. When I was a child dandelions were important to me. I remember blowing off the down to see what time it was. I remember also playing with the stems as little people. I would split the top end with my fingernail and watch it roll up into curls. All my people had madly curling hair.

Before I was old enough for school, and afterwards too, I used to play alone for hours outdoors on our place. Young children today seldom play alone any more, as nearly as I can observe. This is not true of all young children, of course, but of a great many. It is my personal hunch that they are missing something. I recall wandering over our place with no toys in hand. Ours was a pretty stretch of land along the Hudson River, much of it wild, with a large and mysterious cow pasture for a child to explore—a pasture gilded with buttercups in season and dandelions all year.

I remember our land to be a vast tract. Three trees were a forest at my size, a stretch of sunlight a meadow. I had a favorite little path that led through the flowering buddleias and altheas, where I used to watch the ants move over the earth carrying their eggs or bits of leaves, or where I'd build whole villages with small twigs. Another beloved retreat was on top of the cellar window grating behind a mock orange near the coal chute. No one could find me here. Only Delia, our cook, who kept my abode a secret, would pass me cookies up through the grille.

Off in the distance I could hear the comfortable scratchy sound of my father's hoe in the vegetable rows or the squeak of the duster as he dusted the roses. My mother's voice calling my sisters mingled with Delia's Irish songs. The horses neighing in the barn, and the cow mooing in the pasture were all pleasant background noises for my delicious world of make believe—a world so often peopled with dandelion families—mothers, fathers, children—tall, short, fat, thin, and all with curly hair.

Dr. Franz Winkler, noted psychologist and writer, says that children need fantasy and fairy tales in their lives. He says that in America today most children are crammed too full of facts when very young.

"European children have more stars in their eyes," he said recently at a lecture. "Our youngsters," he went on to explain, "seldom have a sufficient world of fantasy to draw on creatively after they grow up."

Perhaps it is the age of production we live in that provides children with so many ready-made toys. Their lives seem surfeited with "things" to the extent that they have very little need to invent or pretend. Why should a piece of wood be a car when a little boy has a whole row of small tin cars? Why should a dandelion be a doll when a little girl has many dolls? Are these children perhaps missing something—and what is happening to their powers of imagination?

Dandelions bring back such glowing childhood memories that, were there any chance of their being permanently eliminated, I would feel desolate—but I don't think this can happen. They are a lusty plant and one of great vigor. A dandelion we have today grows right up out of the bricks on the terrace. It is in a sheltered nook and almost any time from November to April it may send up a flower as well as all summer, of course. One could draw all sorts of moral lessons from this. But moral or not, it is heartening to see a live and growing gold flower on a sunny day when the snow is deep.

April is not only dandelions, it is the Income Tax! I must gather together facts and figures from my part of the budget to help Bob. My husband tells me that he has to be an imaginative detective to figure out some of the things I do in the checkbook. They are quite clear to me, those arrows that go here and there across the page, and the little sign "See back four pages to check number 189," etc. That is, they are clear when I do them. Several weeks later or at Income Tax time when they come to light and Bob asks me about them, I'll confess that it is sometimes difficult to recall. I like figures, though, in spite of the difficulties I often have with them. They are sort of related to the neat, trim rows in the vegetable garden. When I get all confused about anything, I go out and look at those fine, even rows. They help me to unconfuse. So does working in the budget book. But not even the vegetable rows or the budget book could ever clarify me to the point of grasping the essentials of this Income Tax. It is something I'm glad I'm related to only by marriage.

In the midst of gathering our vital facts and the ensuing manoeuvers and slight frenzy as the fatal day approached, Fran sent us a copy of the letter received by the Tax Commissioner of the Central African Federation. I quote:

"Moreover I am not interested in this Income Taxes service of yours. Could you please cancel my name out of your books as this system has upsetted my mind and I do not know who registered me as one of your customers in this matter."

I couldn't agree more.

Aside from the Income Tax another annual indoor indication of spring's arrival is a new hooked rug down on the floor. This spring it is the Unicorn Rug. I started it with Edward III and ended it with the Life of Chaucer—Bob was reading while I was hooking. It is always a great occasion when the last loop is done, the border sewed flat, and the rug is first laid down. The white unicorn is on a green background, surrounded by white leaves and a yellow border. He is so prominent and gay in my bedroom that for the first few days he was there I could see nothing else. I shall miss hooking, but this month I tuck away all the wool strips in moth flakes along with our sweaters and heavy coats. Rug hooking is essentially a winter occupation, and now at long last curtains can be mended and other sewing needs met. I always put these off when I have a rug on the frame because hooking is more fun. I don't know what there is about the process that is so pleasant. When you think about it, it is sort of simple-minded just pulling one little loop after another through the background. But for some reason handling the colors, the pleasant wools, and watching the pattern grow, is soothing. Part of the joy is that Barbara and Dolly think up such enchanting and unique designs. Their rugs all have a contemporary flair, and the colors are bright and cheerful. In this mad world, we could all use a few balance wheels and I guess one of mine is rug hooking.

The new greenhouse is at last complete. We really had a struggle living intimately with orchids for several weeks. The trouble was that they began to pine and languish in spite of everything we could do. There was nothing at all that they liked about our indoor air—too hot and dry, or the shop air—too cold.

Daily our builder faithfully arrived and always in a bright red wool shirt. He decorated the landscape handsomely as he worked, but drove us slightly crazy with his casual creativeness. Each day some great new tangent claimed him and he discovered a much better way of doing things than the way we had specified and he had agreed to at the start. He would decide to have fewer windows, or stain the beautiful natural redwood with a cheap and horrible pinkish stain. He never felt he should bother us with these new ideas, so he just went ahead on his own. At night Bob would discover the errors. Long phone conversations ensued and next day things had to be changed back.

But finally the last glass was set and the last change unchanged, and the orchids, by now decidedly wan, were moved back. I began to wonder how I could revive them. A few were beyond recall from the too cold climate of the shop. The others would hopefully come to life after a few weeks outdoors by the brook where they always summered. But the new greenhouse did look fine—new and fresh and sturdy. What a relief to listen to a good wind or a downpour without feeling that the greenhouse glass top might cave in.

When you first go out and look around the garden in spring, you feel a frenzy of activity come over you. You want to take everything apart and start over. As spring advances, you relax and remember that the means and end are closely related. You flow with the season. Moving more slowly, you catch the rhythm of growing things which never rush, and you find that you are enjoying just being as well as doing.

Laotze says:

> Those who flow as life flows know
> They need no other force:
> They feel no wear, they feel no tear,
> They need no mending, no repair.

Each night you are content because some new outdoor project is complete. Each morning another is begun. It is the response of nature to everything you do that is so rewarding.

Today Bob relaid parts of the brick terrace where it sank last winter. I was uncovering nearby roses and enjoying the light tapping sound of his stone hammer as he placed each brick neatly beside its neighbor. I wheeled the hay from the roses over to mulch the asparagus, and then straightened the bricks that edge the walk through the vegetable garden. It is good to spend almost a whole April day outdoors in air that is fresh and cold. All this particular morning, a great sense of joy filled me. Everything is effortless today. Shoveling compost into the wheelbarrow and wheeling it to the perennial bed in the terrace seems more like a dance than work. The sound of Bob's cultivator later on in the vegetable garden scrunches deliciously. Now and again the metal clinks on a stone, he picks it up and tosses it toward the wall.

This is the time of the waxing moon and we are planting a second crop of spinach and lettuce. Next week during the waning moon we shall be making a second seeding of the underground vegetables, carrots, beets, parsnips, salsify. We follow the old country custom of moon planting and we believe it benefits crops. Anyhow we have a terrific amount of produce, and we enjoy thinking it is partly our cooperating with the moon! And who knows—maybe it is!

We raise vegetables and flowers to nourish our bodies and spirits but whether we are aware of it or not we gardeners plant for another reason. Deep in all of us is a yearning, a basic need for close and intimate contact with the earth. Here with our hands in a warming soil we touch the source of all growth. Here in the live black earth that sifts through the fingers lie the strong forces and basic urges of life itself. Cooperating with wind and rain and sun as we plant and sow, and in a way we don't half understand, we ourselves are replenished and refreshed. A deep need that has been growing in us through the winter is being met.

We cannot sprout a seed, we cannot cause a tree to leaf out, or a brook to flow with spring fullness, but when we do our share we feel nature's response. This first exchange of give and take quickens perceptions that have lain dormant all winter. Moving through the day's activities in and out of the garden, we are filled with a sense of wonder at the annual miracle of spring and our participation in it.

The bright sun shining on the meadow these days has a

clear, clean look. The world seems to have had its face washed. The budding branches of the trees that fringe the meadow and crown Pop's Mountain are bright and sharp against the deep blue sky. I have house trouble. I can't stay indoors. I glance out the window and first thing I know I'm out there moving leaves off the perennials, planting a new miniature rose, sowing radish seeds, or feeding lime to the lilacs.

Each spring I notice something quite new, in fact, each week, each day. Never before have I been so aware of the rich, mellow whistle of the tufted titmouse. Yesterday when I was out his music seemed to come from every tree. These trim little birds with their black beady eyes and perky crests were heralding spring, singing for the joy of it, and probably courting.

In spring I always have to buy a trowel—and for no more reason than that it is spring. This week in Food Fair I succumbed to a wonderful little one with a maple handle and a bright orange spade end. It was so appealing that I bought two more for gardening friends. As I pushed out my wagon the paper towels, cornstarch, onions and cottage cheese were topped by three gay, little orange trowels.

This trowel makes a delightful companion to the one that Bob gave me for Christmas. His is long handled and made of steel, bright and shining. It has the masculine look while this one has the feminine look. Together they will surely see us through the summer. It is fortunate that trowels are only 39¢—I have one weakness at least that is inexpensive.

Easter was a golden morning with the meadow growing greener every moment. The good smell of roasting capons filled the house as I set the table and prepared dinner for Joan and the two boys. Jesse and Bob both have birthdays this month and so the cake said, "Happy Birthday Jesse and Grandpa." A birthday cake only becomes a birthday cake when it has things in it so I had found amusing small items around the house that could be folded up in waxed paper and tucked under the frosting.

All was ready including last year's peas from the freezer when we heard the horn and sounds of merriment. Jesse and Jeff spilled out of the car, Jeff with a skateboard under one arm and a yo-yo in his hand which he was skillfully sending off in all directions. Jesse carried a "flying saucer" and he and Bob promptly took to the field where they tossed this marvelous yellow plastic disc incredible distances between them.

The skateboard was like a giant, wooden roller skate with no harness. It seems you balance both feet on it and coast down hill, steering by throwing your weight. Jeff was very proud of his because it had ball bearings, but it didn't have hubcaps and this worried him.

"It's bad not to have hubcaps, Grandma," he said.

"I'm sure it must be, darling, but why?" I was fixing celery.

"Because the dust from the road gets into the ball bearings. I'll have to make hubcaps while I am here. Do you think Grandpa will let me use his shop?"

"Of course, darling, I'm sure he would."

A few moments later, "Grandma," Jeff said, "I have a present for you."

"Yes?"

Jeff carefully took a long, slim fold of paper out of his pocket and I stopped scraping celery while he opened it to reveal six sparklers. I've always been partial to sparklers. My father loved them, too, and would bring them home for us four children to light most any time of year. He was as excited as we to watch them burn. One year when Bob Jr. returned from Korea I put sparklers in his birthday cake instead of candles. They were not only glamorous and sensational but nearly set the house on fire. I always felt they were well worth the burned spot in the red kitchen counter that we have lived with ever since.

Now in Jeff's hand lay six.

"Jeff, they are perfectly lovely," I said, "and I do thank you."

"Shall I keep them for you?" he asked, "they'd be very safe in my pocket and whenever you need one you can have it."

"Of course," I replied, "you keep them."

"I have a present for Grandpa, too."

Through the window I saw Bob with a long reach catch the flying saucer, and Joan nearby was gathering daffodils. Jeff was bursting with his secret present for Bob and I could see he was going to have to share it with me ahead of time.

He fished in another pocket and brought out another paper.

"This is something very useful," he said, and opened it to reveal six, short, black firecrackers, each slim as a match.

"I thought you wouldn't like the noise, but I knew Grandpa would. These are so useful because, you see, they are small and fit easily into a pocket and he can carry them around. When he needs a firecracker, he will always have one."

"They *are* wonderful, Jeff, and Grandpa will love them I'm sure," I said, getting the celery and olives on the table while Jeff was wrapping up the firecrackers again.

What a day with flying saucers, skateboards, presents, cake, and "useful" firecrackers.

We all laughed over the little items in the cake—seeds, a tiny toy tree obviously symbolizing the new dogwoods, paper clips, a dime, polished pebbles, and sea shells.

After dinner we went to Compo Beach for the great moment of flying the Christmas kite the first time. At long last we had in hand 1100 yards of monofilament nylon line that tested to 50 lbs. Although it had turned cold and windy, nothing could keep us from sending up the kite on its virgin trip. It took two to launch it. The kite spun restlessly in Jeff's arms and the moment he let it go it took off and up while Bob unreeled the string. The great colorful wings caught the wind and carried it high into a gray sky. It was beautiful to see the giddy pink wings riffle in the breeze. We all took turns holding the string to "feel the wind."

Compo was gay with all sizes and colors of kites—we counted ten. After a while we drew the kite in and headed for home. Joan and Jesse drove off, but Jeff stayed on. This was his week for a visit—and a wonderful week it was. A day in New York, a day lunching with my sister Connie in Riverdale, and plenty of exploring by car and on foot. Every night while I got dinner Jeff sat on the red stool in the kitchen and read to me from a fascinating book about otters, *Ring of Bright Water.*

I had to leave him one day to give a talk in Bedford. When I got back with cookies tied up in my purse for him, he was in a fine glow and the study was knee-deep in newspapers, glue, bits of copper, and the large metal shears. He had found some old pieces of copper in the shop and had made hubcaps for the skateboard.

"Nobody in my class, Grandma, will have copper hubcaps," he said happily.

Actually, they were very neat and handsome and I'm sure "useful" and important! Later on we walked up to Mrs. Glover's for eggs. Coming back down the hill, he coasted circles around me on the skateboard while I walked sedately along the road.

On Jeff's last night we were waiting for Bob to come. Dinner simmered quietly on the stove. We were walking around outside the house in the gloaming, appreciating the last of the sunset and looking about at spring's beginnings.

"Let's burn the last sparklers," Jeff said drawing two out of his pocket. We had burned the rest during the week but had saved these for a great occasion. Standing by the front door we each held one and lit them. With a delicate sparkling sound rich streams of bright gold stars danced off the two slim pieces of metal. For a few delicious moments they shone their magic in the gathering dusk. As the two sticks turned dull red and went out, we heard the car drive in at the far end of the lane. Simultaneously a sound echoed from the north meadow—the first whippoorwill of the season.

5

May is the time of growth

MAY SWEEPS IN on a theme of daffodils. I gather armfuls from the meadow and next day so many more unfold that I cannot see where I have picked. Along the roadside the willows are tumbled masses of pale green foam, and forsythia, in streaming fountains of flowers, reflects the sun's golden rays. Here a dusty pink weeping cherry adds a soft note of color. There a magnolia tree is a bouquet of pink blossoms, and everywhere maples are shaking out their tight fists of green into lacy new leaves.

Spring may officially begin on March 22nd, but for me it began yesterday when Bob hung the hammock. Our rope hammock is from South Carolina with touches of southern leisure woven into its strands. We set up the porch, laid down the new grass rug from the Philippines that feels like thatch and smells like a meadow. Gay porch covers and cushions emerged from their winter bags, and in the late afternoon sunlight we sat there for the first time this season.

In the vegetable garden the peas, a fresh, bright green, march row on row across the earth. Furry lines of carrots grow beside the tiny beet seedlings. The latter, though scarcely visible, indicate their future color in the thread-like red stems, and the red-tinted leaves, tiny as a pinhead. For the first time in our lives parsnips came up. One of my organic gardening friends had said to water the seeds as soon as we sowed. Now they are thick as grass. Equally thick are the turnips which sprouted in a week.

This time of year so much happens that you hate to miss a move. Every day, every hour, something in the garden grows an inch. Asparagus ripens so rapidly you can almost see it rise up while you watch. We pick every spear that is ready one night and by the next there is another meal waiting. One day, standing at the window, I realize that the meadow grass has grown long enough for the wind to ripple.

The rug hookers, who become a sewing group in summer, will be here this week, and it couldn't be a better time. The spring wild flowers are in their prime. Meadow parsnips gild the field. The wood betony, a gypsy plant with tousled corollas, is full out, and in contrast comes the prim lavender daisy-like robin's plantain. Wild lily of the valley stretches through the shadows, and forget-me-nots border our stream. Along the banks Virginia bluebells nod, while edging the woodland path twenty-one pink lady slippers stand in graceful shyness. Everywhere ferns are uncurling, the feathery royal fern that you must feel every time you walk by, the hay-scented fern, and the New York fern whose fronds taper at both ends, named for the New Yorkers who burn their candles at both ends.

The three dogwood trees planted last month all flowered and are now covered with healthy leaves. We've won the battle of the leaf rollers on the roses by picking, burning, squashing, spraying. We spray the roses once or twice in May, and with luck and ladybugs to eat the aphids, not again. Our lilacs too are perfect now. Lilacs are May in essence. Each lovely lavender spray is full out halfway up but the tip is still in bud, giving both fulfillment and promise together. In its rampant growth May becomes the fulfillment of spring, and at the same time, the promise of summer.

While May is the distillation of all that is lovely everywhere outdoors, it is the season of little gnats too! One minute you are in a state of delight at the world in general and the spot where you stand in the garden in particular, and the next you are in a halo of almost invisible tiny black creatures who haven't eaten since the world began! Life, at times, is somewhat like this, an interesting combination of gnats and delights. We must need gnats or they wouldn't be here, though I have often wondered why. Possibly the bothering insects in our lives, whatever form and shape they take, represent the shadow side of things. How often we think things are "just great if only—" or "why did this have to happen just now—and to me?" The need may be to accept and come to terms with these "if only's" and make our peace with them. We obviously must face whatever problem comes but we needn't attach to it or linger with it. It is better when we can see through and beyond, work through and beyond.

This week Bob cut the lawn for the first time and the delicious scent of fresh grass mingles with other May fragrances. I enjoy listening to the putt putt of the mower, and the slicing sound as he sharpens the sickle and trims edges. We mow only a twelve foot wide strip around the house and paths through the meadow to places we like to go. The rest of the land is uncut flowering fields, woods, and streams. It takes exactly one half hour a week to mow this lawn.

Its care and upkeep are brief and simple. Lawns are not among the things we worry about, and we refuse to get excited about crab grass. I realize it has become a thriving and prosperous business to eliminate crab grass and quite a pastime for some. If you enjoy working at it, more power to you. In the general scheme of things it doesn't seem very important to us whether a lawn has some crab grass in it or not.

What, after all, is the purpose of a lawn? A green lawn attractively frames a house. It is a pleasant place to sit during the summer; grass feels good on bare feet, whether you are six or sixty; a stretch of grass is a fine spot from which to fly a kite. Trees, shrubs, and flower beds rise gracefully from this area of green. You can enjoy all these aspects of a lawn even if it is not thoroughbred grass. There are many things in life one has to take drastic action about, but crab grass is not on our list. I get much more stirred up about beer cans tossed into sweeps of wild geraniums along the roadside.

Some days you want to be in a variety of places all at once—relaxing in the hammock, scratching the soil loose around young perennials, walking through the meadow, or perhaps just watching the bird feeders and the different visitors—the cardinal, the tufted titmouse, and the goldfinch.

Every morning a bluebird perches among the apple blossoms that cover the tree thick as popcorn. At dusk a thrush sings from down the valley, and the little warblers and "witchety" birds squeak along the brook. Now and again a robin puffs with pride as he struts across the green grass, head cocked, listening for a worm. All the birds are full of business. Leave a length of yarn or string on the terrace and in an hour it is gone. The responsibilities of householding are uppermost. We keep watch to see who is building where. The phoebes are settling over the door to the shop. At one point several feet of nylon line trailed down from the nest they were building. I thought someone might inadvertently catch this and pull the carefully made structure apart, so I cut it off where it dangled.

I should have had more confidence in the phoebe, who knew exactly what she was doing. By night the remaining loose end had been woven up into the nest. Had she counted on the part I took off? How often we human beings interfere where we have no business—and help in areas where help is not needed.

What birds say seems to be a matter of who is listening. One friend in advertising insists that our whippoorwill in the gloaming chants "*Ches*-ter-*field, Ches*-ter-*field*." But when we returned from Switzerland last summer this same whippoorwill quite clearly said, "*Wel*-come-*home, Wel*-come-*home*." The barred owl obviously calls "Who cooks for you—who cooks for *you* all?" What the little wren has to tell when he perches on top of a garden post in the bright sunlight is beyond words. In some way he communicates his mood of joy and ecstasy and we quicken in response to fresh green everywhere, to a warming sun, and to merely being alive at the moment and listening to a small wren.

One sunny morning when the grass was heavy with dew and the mourning doves calling, our pair of wild ducks flew over. They fly together, one a little ahead of the other. Is it the gentleman always leading the lady? Then there comes a time when I see only one flying over and I know that they have chosen their nesting site and the lady is sitting on eggs. These ducks come back every year and raise a family somewhere along our stream. I have never found the nest, but I have never looked very hard, feeling they should be granted the privacy they have sought.

Orioles also return every year. One day I watched the female high in the swinging branch of an elm create a nest like a hammock. I forgot everything I was supposed to be doing, and with the glasses observed how she wove each strand skillfully into the whole while the nest gradually took shape.

As she worked her mate came and went, and his rich mellow song filled the air. An oriole just naturally makes a certain kind of nest because it is an oriole. How different the homemaking ideas of the great horned owl who builds of sticks and bark, or the hummingbird who settles on an apple branch and lines his nest with down from the uncurling fronds of a cinnamon fern.

I went out into the garden this morning with no plan. Sometimes this is the most enjoyable way—merely to go out and see what has grown in the night, what has happened everywhere. I have scissors in my pocket, and raffia too. After last night's rain the cocoa bean mulch on the flower beds smells of the chocolate fudge my father used to make. I picked a few buttercups from the meadow and arranged an airy fairy bouquet in a pewter bowl. From now till frost we shall continually have flowers on the dining table.

Over in the vegetable garden the lettuces were beautiful, so crisp and neat. On the right side of the path marched a row of romaine, upright and formal, on the left salad bowl, ruffled and frilled.

Elsie, to Bob's dismay, has cleaned out the fireplace again. He always sighs when this happens. A good fire builder must have a bed of ashes to build on and we will be having more fires. But Elsie does save these ashes for the garden. Removing the old nails, but leaving black ends of charcoal, I spread them around the roses and delphiniums. A few weeds in the perennials next invited pulling. These days I hate to wash the garden soil off my hands. If I am staying outside and not getting a meal I don't and it dries, and flakes off leaving a tight sensation at my fingertips that I rather like—it is so much a part of outdoors and gardening.

Here on the trellis clematis swings loose and needs tying. Raffia is not only decorative but it seems right to be tying up plants with nature-made dried grass rather than man-made string. I also like to handle raffia. We keep a hank on the terrace on a peg, along with a scratcher and trowel. Everything is there and handy when needed.

I must tie the lily too. We have one magnificent Auratum lily in the perennial bed that produced thirteen flowers last summer. Our single lily reminds me of the story of the famous chrysanthemum grower in Japan who, when he learned that the Emperor was coming for a viewing of his prize flowers, cut off all but one solitary perfect bloom. The Orientals who stress quality in gardening rather than quantity have a point of view worth considering. We vary this theme by *planting* quality instead of quantity. When we want hundreds of anything we naturalize it and let nature tend it, otherwise we set out few and choice plants, and only one each of certain perennials. This way is more carefree, but more than this, sometimes you really see and appreciate one flower more than a dozen. I could not enjoy a dozen lilies any more than our single perfect one.

Our tulips are all out now. I have a particular feeling about these blossoms too. The great huge tulips that you encounter in flower shows, I'll admit, are a horticultural achievement, but when it comes to tulips as large as grapefruit, I'll take grapefruit! I prefer tulips normal size, and each year, since we don't take them out of the ground, the blooms grow more numerous but a little smaller. The small ones are equally lovely.

In May our tulips in the little six by twelve perennial bed are sensational. I counted sixty out just now. They open every morning in the sun and fold at night. In the morning they face east and all day long they follow the sun with a slight inclination of the heads until, when it sets behind Pop's Mountain, they are tilted westward.

I like the way the white tulips often develop pink edges after a few days. I like the whole range of lavenders, oranges, reds, yellows, and white. Arrange a few of them in a vase in graceful curves, and to your surprise next morning they have altered their positions and created a new design. Your arrangement never stays arranged your way.

There is a pleasant old English legend about tulips. In Devon the old folks say that fairies used to cradle their babies in the flower cups while they danced all night in the light of the moon. The goddess Flora, observing this, gave tulips, which until then had been drab, their brilliant colors of today. It was gay tinted petals that, each moonlight eve thereafter, received their charges!

Another favorite flower legend is about dogwood, also a feature of a New England May.

At the time of Christ's crucifixion, the dogwood, so runs the tale, was a tree as mighty as the oak. The cross upon which Christ died was made from its wood. According to the story, Jesus sensed the distress of the timbers over their cruel role, and told the dogwood that, because of its sorrow, and compassion for his suffering, it should henceforth grow slim and bent and twisted. Never again could a dogwood be used to form a cross. Jesus also decreed that the tree would bear blossoms, each one shaped like a cross. There would be two long and two short petals, and a "crown of thorns" in the center of each blossom. At the outer edges their petals would ever after carry the stigmata, brown as rust and blood, so each person viewing dogwood would remember.

In the early morning before seven the world is a very special place. Today I was out by six—the temperature was forty and I could see my breath. The air was crisp and clear, like air at a high altitude. There is something private about the early morning. By seven neighbors are stirring, and we must share the world. Cars pass down Valley Forge Road and another day begins. But that morning at six the world was mine, and nothing intruded. With a bushel basket I settled in the vegetable garden among the neat rows of beets and parsley, loosening the soil around small seedlings. On all sides nature was wide awake. The cardinal was blending his song with the music of the robin. A catbird was greeting the sunny morning, the gargling notes of the red-wing blackbird sounded across the valley, while nearby a fat, nubbly toad blinked at me.

At first the earth was chilly, my fingertips felt numb. Icy cold drops of dew hung on every leaf, and a silvery world shone with the freshness of a new day. It was pleasant thinning and taking out tiny weeds. The soil was filled with worms—a good sign always. For an hour I enjoyed the quietness, my nearness to earth, and the friendly toad. Gradually the soil warmed, as the sun warmed, and I no longer saw my breath. After a while I heard the neighbors stirring. Bob would soon be up. Back in the kitchen while I was preparing breakfast the kettle spoke, the icebox purred, the furnace also had things to say, and I listened. I welcomed the lovely fragrance of fresh toast that filled the room, and the aroma of sizzling bacon that mingled with the coffee scent. Right on the heels of our most romantic moments we are quite likely to get hungry! And so life balances us between earth and heaven. In man these two worlds meet and blend.

The first thing after breakfast I planted the moon flowers along the wall of the shop. By midsummer they would be a curtain of green starred with myriads of snowy flowers. The fabulous blossoms open at dusk each night. While you stand and watch, the long pointed buds, one after another, visibly uncurl, and creased white petals shake out into deeply fragrant satiny flowers.

I had dropped the hard-as-a-pebble round seeds in water after filing a little nick in each one. Now forty-eight hours later these seeds were completely transformed. Each one was at least three times its original size, slightly lumpy, and with cracks over the surface. In handling them one of the shells slipped off, revealing a pair of tightly folded waxy white leaves ready and waiting to grow. I like all seeds—how different they are, the cornflower from the pea, the zinnia from the snapdragon. But all seeds have in common an outer coating of some sort and a germ of life within waiting to grow.

Wu Ming Fu, a twelfth century poet and philosopher, wrote:

> The seed that is to grow
> must lose itself as seed;

And they that creep
may graduate through
chrysalis to wings.

Wilt thou then, O mortal,
cling to husks which
falsely seem to you
the self?

I like his thought that we need to shed our "husks" to grow. And, of course, if we resist needed change then life itself tears off our shells and we grow willy nilly. As a wise friend of ours once said, "We are like teabags and sometimes must get into hot water to know our own strength!"

On Sunday Bob and Janet, our neighbor, and I set out on our favorite walk up towards Indian Meadow, past the spring, on to the dam, over Pop's Mountain and home. This was such a different kind of walk from our deer-hunting one in the snow last winter. Today a shiny white light filtered down through dim areas where the forest was dense. It fell on green and growing hemlocks, and giant fallen logs blanketed with bright yellow-green moss. Cushions of gray reindeer moss, fairy cups, and red-tipped lichen spread through the meadow, and here and there a dead tree stood out silver against the live and thriving spruce and pine. As we neared the reservoir we could hear the sound of water lapping the shore, and the greening earth felt springy underfoot.

A few chickadees followed, hopping in and out of the branches along the path, curious no doubt about these great creatures that intruded upon their world. Curious they were, but friendly, too. They reminded me of Bob's phoebe last fall. This little bird followed him about all one week-end as he was working around the place. The bird kept lighting on something a few feet away. He grew bolder and closer till he perched on the wheelbarrow as Bob was filling it with orchids to bring into the greenhouse. I wonder where that particular phoebe has been all winter and if he will return and remember Bob this spring.

It was pleasant climbing through the woods, stepping from rock to rock and feeling the brush of hemlock branches as we pushed through a stand of them. Here and there we would break off a new green hemlock tip to chew. These taste a little like spruce gum and are said to be filled with Vitamin C. Soft moss everywhere felt fresh and alive. Here a huge old chestnut lay flat and rotting. Young saplings were leafing out around it. The partly disintegrated old tree was contributing nourishment to the slim new ones. Surely we also are fed, nourished, and replenished by our families, what they were and what they stood for.

You learn a lot about people when you take them walking in the woods. Some stride along wrapped in their own concerns. Others feel the woods and reach out to the wonder of them. At times we all enter the woods with things preying on our minds. An hour in the forest, though, usually brings a kind of peace and clear vision often lacking in the midst of crowds and activities. Sometimes we start out speaking of everyday affairs, and after a few minutes the pauses in the conversation grow longer. The wood itself begins to speak and we fall silent. The sounds of a stream, of the wind in the treetops, the whir of a startled woodcock flying off, all seem more important than what we might say.

There is a certain place in the woods that we call our "Green Mansions" spot. W. H. Hudson would have loved it. We like to introduce friends to this area. The tumbled logs are furred with moss and the gray rocks covered with designs in lichen. The brown earth floor is scattered over with leaves and ferns. The first hepaticas open here in April, starry-eyed and fresh. Today we found rattlesnake plantain with its patterned sage-green leaves. In a beam of sunlight clumps of dutchman's-breeches spread around rocks. The sound of tumbling water drew us to golden marsh marigolds by the hundreds. Everywhere tight pink laurel buds were swelling.

Early May days in the spring woods are precious to us three. This will be our last walk here for a while. We have seen the pair of black snakes that lives in one of our meadow walls and this means that we cannot climb here any longer because of the possibility of a chance encounter with a copperhead. These woods are for exploring from October to May but never from May to October. During the spring and summer we walk in other places.

Walking is a fairly recent pastime for both of us. We never used to walk much until about six years ago. It was at an annual physical check-up that the doctor said I should walk. Bob, he said, must walk, too, since he sat in an office all day.

Gardening, badminton, swimming, shopping, house cleaning, were none of them the same, the doctor assured me.

"I mean walking with no basket of leaves to carry, no vacuum in hand. I want you simply to walk with no purpose, no goal other than walking, and seeing what is around you. This you must do a minimum of a mile a day, two, if possible."

Up to that time I thought I knew our valley and its people. After all, we had lived here a number of years and driven many times over the nearby roads. The houses and gardens of a few special friends we did know well and one or two other spots. But when we first commenced to walk we discovered a whole new world and all within a few miles of home.

Now when I see streams of cars hastening over the roads and so few people on foot, when I see children waiting at corners for the school bus, for parents to taxi them, or to ask for a lift, I suspect that as a nation we are forgetting how to walk. At least we have that reputation.

One day on a Swiss Alp we paused beside the trail to talk to a European couple who were amazed to find that we were Americans.

"But Americans never walk!" they explained.

That first day after the visit to the doctor I thought walking was going to be a great nuisance as I reluctantly dragged myself from some lettuce seedlings I was transplanting. Dutifully I headed down the road—the same road on which I had driven hundreds of times to town. My thoughts were of lettuces, more pansies I would plant by the front door, and I must remember to call about the stove to be fixed. But it was a sunny May day and gradually these concerns sloughed off. The first thing I noticed was a last year's cardinal's nest in an evergreen beside the road. How many times had I driven past here, totally oblivious to the young birds hatching. And now that pair of cardinals was back. For a few moments they inspected the old nest and apparently decided on a new one. They explored several other branches, and on my way back had already started weaving this year's home.

Had this brook always run under the road just here? Beside it stood a snowy drift of white flowers. I brought one home and identified it as toothwort—wonderful names wild flowers have!

The delights of the road on my first walk drew me on and on. Lettuces and stoves drifted totally out of mind. That spring I learned to recognize fifty different varieties of wild flowers and all less than a mile away. I also kept track of that cardinal's nest and was present the morning the young birds first tried their wings. The road to town is no longer merely the road to town. It has become my garden and I observe seasonal changes there as affectionately as in the flower beds on our terrace.

When you speed along in the car what do you know of the melody of a brook? Wind in meadow grass? The humming of bees in the clover? The subtle differences of bird songs, the crackle of someone's brush fire? As you walk each of your five senses seems to sharpen. There are the smells of the countryside which you never notice behind car windows, the fragrance of wild honeysuckle and the drifting scent of pear blossoms over someone's hedge.

One day I suddenly became aware of the earth through my sneakers and it wasn't a hole either! The ground had a fine, firm feel, and I was enjoying this. A lightness came into each step and moving became effortless. We often think about our bodies when we have a pain somewhere. Less often do we become conscious of them in the process of normal activity such as walking. I find true pleasure in the sensation of my body moving along the road, and in the free swing of my arms.

Bob soon caught the spirit of walking and became as enthusiastic as I. We first discovered the magic of early morning wandering along the shore near Compo where shadows are long, footprints are deep blue, and beach grass swirls lazy circles in the sand.

Our new world included the world at night. After dark we met glowworms like straying stars caught by the side of the road. Our flashlight revealed each to be a little crusty, segmented worm, who sparkled as he wove his way through the leaves. Down the road from us Mr. Follett has a plant nursery. For years we have driven past him kneeling among his beautiful rows of perennials and pulling weeds. Now I stop for a few moments and we compare notes on outwitting the coons. I learn the best methods of storing carrots for the winter. His sound practical philosophy comes over the stone wall. Instead of just a kneeling figure to fly by at lots of miles an hour, he and his wife have become our friends.

It wasn't easy to start walking a mile a day. At first days would slide by and I had even forgotten that I had forgotten to walk. I used to think I hadn't time to build in this new habit, but actually walking has brought both Bob and me a greater sense of leisure. It has also brought us a whole new world that lies right around us—a world of beauty and of wonder—a place whose horizons stretch far and wide, outwardly and inwardly.

Our family from California has arrived—Bob and Susan and two-year-old Miles. Life is instantaneously transformed. The high stool in the kitchen has become a garage beneath whose tall red legs a number of small cars cluster. Little bright-colored tin or plastic automobiles grow up out of the flower beds and vegetable rows. The living room cushions have trouble remaining in their accustomed places on the sofa. When you are two it is much more fun to slide along the floor on cushions than to lean against them on the sofa. The icebox is full of milk and the clothesline constantly waves cheerfully colored small garments in the breeze.

Every morning after breakfast I have an assistant gardener. While our son and his wife eat their breakfast, I take young Miles by the hand and we go out to garden. He is all interest and curiosity. One day we discover the furry buds on the Oriental poppies have split to reveal streaks of scarlet. Another day the first rose opens. We meet a fat earthy toad and angleworms become a sensation. It is difficult to imagine being so young that you don't know about buttercups and a golden chin, and liking butter. I hold a buttercup up to Miles' chin, and at first he is suspicious. All of a sudden he approves, reaches out for the flower and streaks back to the house to see if his father likes butter. Communication with a two-year-old has to reach beyond words, which are often only half understood. It is a rather wonderful age because Miles is an open book with moods right on the surface. Tears and laughter, frustration and content are all right there together, and you can't be sure which will turn on or off at any given moment. You can only know that you will be surprised, and sometimes even horrified.

It is thought-provoking to realize that this youngster may perhaps stand on the moon, and yet right now he doesn't know the names of half the things in this world. Thinking back to the time when I didn't know about birds' nests and eggs, or frogs in streams, or seeds to plant, or that buttercups made your chin yellow, is impossible. In the fascinating process of introducing this small boy to the whole world of nature I catch brief glimpses of things through his eyes, and share in his wonder.

On sunny days the new kite lures us all to the shore. Lying in the lea of the stone wall, for it is still chilly, we send it aloft and anchor the line with a large rock. It is pleasantly relaxing stretched out there with the colorful kite rippling in the breeze overhead, and it is a good time for leisure talk. Letters are wonderful, but how fine to learn firsthand of the goals, ambitions, and activities of our son and his wife. As we exchanged ideas now and again one of us would reach up and hold the string a moment to feel the wind up high and the kite motion.

It is a joy to watch our small golden-haired two-year-old in a diminuitive red bathing suit splash through the shallow edge of the waves as he drags his bright red boat behind him. When Miles tires of this we build castles in the sand. At any age there is something all absorbing about running your hands through wet sand and building mounds and roads and tunnels. We make a moat around the castle, and a drawbridge, and the moat fills with sea water. Small bits of shell are people up in the towers. Miles has no idea what castles are, or princesses or kings, but he is soon speaking these unfamiliar new words as if they are part of his life. He pushes shells up and down the sand roads pretending they are cars, unaware of the amusing anachronism. Pretty soon a wave comes and takes away our castle and road and moat. The kingdom is lost—we retreat to higher ground and begin over.

What is it about a castle that appeals to adult and child alike? At times we all like to go inside our personal castles, close the gates and pull up the drawbridge. The important thing is to sense this need and respond to it before it becomes too great. Perhaps even more important is to be able to know when the other person in your life is in his castle with the drawbridge up, and to respect his needs.

It has taken me years to accept Bob's silent times, and not intrude. I used to be hurt and wonder what I had done or said wrong. Then I realized I had the same need. Sometimes I like to remove myself physically from all activities and people for an hour or a day. Bob, on the other hand, moves within himself and becomes quiet. At these times he is in his castle and impregnable. His physical self may be among us, but his spirit is miles away and wants to be.

A withdrawal period for anyone can be a source of true refreshment and replenishment, whether it is gardening alone at sunrise or a silent retreat inward when with people.

All during May we are constantly aware of things changing, daily, hourly, as they grow and develop. This is the month that you *know,* and even the greatest skeptic begins to suspect, that there lies at the core of things something quite apart from man's restless endeavors, something that remains unperturbed by man's wildest tamperings with earth and sky. While you watch spring come and participate as a gardener in this period of great growth, you keenly sense a rhythm that is greater than your own. Beneath and beyond the urgencies of May lies a steadying force, a balance for moments when the world seems to have gone mad and to be heading you know not whither.

Somewhat wistfully we loose and let May go—it has been an excitingly beautiful month—a time of flowers and fragrances, of brilliant color, and of expanding life everywhere.

6

June and the earth burgeons

JUNE COMES and the burgeoning land is fragrant with the scent of a million flowers. Cherries swing high on their branches; great flat heads of elderberry blooms drape over bushes where dark blueberries will ripen later. Nature in her richest mood flings colors, blossoms, and fruit over the earth. Wild strawberries tint the meadow. On sunny noons the scent mingles with that of the spicy peony blossoms. My fingers are not green this month, but pink tipped, for I must wander down several times a day to taste the sugar-sweet berries. Are wild strawberries particularly choice because each single one is only a morsel and you never have anywhere near enough?

There is an urgency in April and May in both man and Nature, an urgency that quiets during June. The promises of early spring are fulfilled this month. In the garden everything is in and up—all basic work complete, and we relax while the curtain rises on summer. This is the month we spread our deep hay mulch and after that the garden becomes entirely carefree—no more tending or weeding. This leaves hammock time, beach time, visiting time, hours of wonderful long conversations with friends on vast or simple subjects, and best of all, time to do nothing.

Some people feel that doing nothing and being bored relate.

Boredom is a word I don't especially know, seldom use, and never think of as a state I experience. If it means a do-nothing interval between activities, I'm sure we all need a little more "boredom" in our lives. Certainly we all need more spaces between events! I'd not call such a space boredom, however, but rather a period in which to absorb and deepen the happening immediately behind you and prepare for the one that lies ahead.

Robert Paul Smith, author of the delightful book about children, *Where Did You Go? Out—What Did You Do? Nothing!* says, "Boredom is a judgment you make on yourself. Doing nothing is a state of being,"—and an enviable state, I'll add. Our days can be too full of a number of things. We'd all be happy as kings, I think, if our lives weren't quite so crowded. Now, in June all courses and winter commitments have ended. Group activities and community endeavors declare a holiday. We can thin our weeks even further, and frequently for a day, for an hour, do nothing—just nothing at all.

One soft fragrant June afternoon I settled on the terrace to read and after a few moments found myself no longer seeing the page of print and not even thinking. My mind purely drifted. Through the meadow the grass swung feathery tops in the breeze. A few feet off a ruby-throated humming-bird hovered in mid-air before the delphinium. He sipped nectar from a sky-blue floret, and I wondered what the flavor of a delphinium was, and how it differed from the taste of the dianthus where he next darted. How lovely to watch a hummingbird and not feel I should be doing something else. These last weeks our days move in a slower, gentler tempo—a tempo that leaves us more open generally.

The sound of the birds on the ground gathering food for their newly hatched young is a subtle sound. The fragrance of a fresh green meadow at noon is a subtle scent. The scurrying of a little mouse across the grass and into a hole is a small event. But such sounds, scents, and small happenings are part of the flow and continuity of nature and relating to them in the pauses of the day can be a source of true replenishment.

During these treasured interludes of calm we may also just possibly receive added insights about our own selves. We may come to know better this person called I.

It is good and necessary to learn how to do—to accomplish—to be efficient. But it is equally vital to learn how to *be*—how to turn off the mind and do nothing. Wise is the man or woman who knows when one is needed, and when the other.

I believe that since the last insect book was published Nature has invented a new bug. One morning I was standing in the midst of our dianthus watching the butterflies drift over the delicately fringed flowers. First a swallow-tailed butterfly came and then several other varieties, and finally there arrived a fabulous creature that I am sure Nature had just invented. He was brown and orange, perhaps two inches long. His body seemed to have a sort of felt or velvet covering. He had two feelers and a third long, marvelous one emerging from the center of his head. This he inserted into each blossom and sucked the nectar out. He hovered in the air like a hummingbird while he dined, and his wings beat so furiously fast that you couldn't see them but only hear them hum.

He isn't in any of our insect books. What can he be—just

one of Nature's interesting insolubles? (I found out later he was a hummingbird moth.)

I hate to go indoors these days, even for a drink of water, lest I miss something wonderful like this bug, or a new rose opening, or another Oriental poppy out. We have twenty-eight buds on one poppy plant. Each morning several split the seams of their furry skins, toss them off, and stretch petals out to full size. In a newly opened poppy, the purple-black stamens dusted with pollen tremble in the slightest zephyr, and the flower has a glorious sheen, a pristine loveliness. An hour later the pollen has spilled over the scarlet petals, brushing them with dark streaks. They are still beautiful but different.

Another feature in the perennial bed right now is the combination of pyrethrum and inky blue veronica next to each other. The former is deep carmine, so bright in the sun you can scarcely look, the latter, the electric blue of little Cape Cod ponds in late October. Growing together they are a sensation.

What a pleasure it is to toss hay about. As soon as Bob left this morning I went out into the garden with the hay fork, which in itself is a nice object. The slim, gracefully curved prongs are a joy to look at. Our pile of fragrant hay stands over by the stone wall. Bob Harper, the keeper of the reservoir and the trimmer of the sides of the road, dumped it there a few days ago for us to use as mulch. Some is dry and hay-colored, the rest is still a live green. After last night's rain the earth is damp and this is the time to mulch. I spread the hay by hand along the rows between the beets, onions, carrots, parsnips and chard. I snugged it up close to the slim blue-green onion stalks, flattened it along the path on the rows where we walk, and all the while it was light and enjoyable to handle—and very fragrant. A scent can take you traveling back many years and the scent of hay always reminds me of the hayloft of my youth where I used to play with friends, and where a family of cats and kittens always lived.

Today there were a few brown sticks in among the hay, and I kept a sharp lookout for snakes. One time last year we were spreading hay together and Bob inadvertently picked up a copperhead on the fork along with the hay. I'd been carrying hay by the armfuls up to that moment. We proceeded more slowly and watchfully thereafter.

I was in the leather shop in Westport this morning getting a purse repaired when all of a sudden a hush fell over customers and sales people alike. Conversation ceased. We all listened to the radio. "Four—three—two—one," and now the space rocket Gemini 4 was off. I'm sure everyone else must have felt with me a kind of tingling. In the looks we strangers exchanged was a great unspoken prayer for the safety of these two men, for the success of the venture, and a sense of how their families must be feeling. For a split second there flashed from person to person in the store an unspoken exchange, a shared concern which brought us all close.

I used to think—really, now here we are reaching for the moon when we had better solve some of the knotty problems on earth first—illness, poverty, hunger.

But my point of view is altering. Surely earth problems should be solved, and worked on steadily, but people will always reach out beyond familiar frontiers, will always stretch towards the unknown. The mountain has to be climbed because it is there. Perhaps it is good for nations to race each other into space rather than to marshall all these same forces along with hate, greed, and the cruelty of one human being to another in a war against each other.

When I go to an organic garden club meeting I never know what will occur! I can only be sure that it will be something unusual and that most likely I will come home with an uneasy feeling about what the government is or is not doing, and immediately I'll have to send off letters to Senators and the President.

This particular meeting was no exception. It was at Virginia Gund's on a perfectly beautiful day with everything green and fragrant, with lots of blue sky and white clouds and the hawkweed coming into flower. First we all admired the completely charming herb garden. In fact, it was rather difficult to go into the house for the meeting after walking through the vegetable garden, around the meadow, and pinching and smelling all the herbs. The herbs border a little curving path that leads to a reflecting pool and I would never tire of wandering there. Among the neat orderly plants any weed which inadvertently popped up would die of shame!

The refreshments at the Organic Garden Club consisted of rose hip and camomile tea and Shrewsbury cakes, which are crisp little cookies made of roses and simply delicious. It is always great to see everybody and to exchange news on how we are coping with aphids on the roses, and compare notes on how tall our various vegetables are. The uneasy note, this time, is the fluoridation bill that passed in Connecticut last week. Many of the members are filled with dire predictions and one or two avidly working for a repeal. It seems the bill won't come into effect for a couple of years so I imagine we will hear a lot about it at coming meetings. The subject of this session was honey and roses and we learned plenty.

I also met Mary Hill, a new member, who offered me some sweet potato plants. I drove her home after the meeting to get them. She is rather a remarkable young woman with seven children from 13 years to four weeks, seven puppies, and a house with seven bedrooms! Just thinking of seven children of those ages filled me with admiration for this capable, gay, attractive, young mother who seemed so happy and in control of her life and herself. We wandered through her 70 x 125 vegetable garden—all organic—and she sent me home with a bundle of sweet potato plants. Of course we have absolutely no room to plant them, but I do love sweet potatoes. That evening Bob solved their location—between a row of corn and the tomatoes. I put them in a pail of water to soak for the night before setting them out.

June is the beginning of summer and all beginnings are thrilling. A beginning is always a challenge, too. Who knows what this season will bring—corn and coons?—swimming and sunbathing?—thunderstorms and vacations?—excitements and disappointments? Some of all, no doubt.

In June wherever you look the rich green of abundant growth spreads over the landscape. Lie in the hammock and gaze up through the maple tree overhead. Myriads of overlapping green leaves, shot through with sunlight, flicker as the branches stir. How many thousands of leaves there are on each tree. Who could even count them? They seem almost to push each other off the twigs. In the meadow the flowers and blades of grass are so thick they all but snatch the soil space from each other!

The deep, beautiful, purple clematis trails eager tendrils from the top of its post looking for something higher to climb. The grapevine stretches out arms of green to clasp the house roof in a firm embrace. And along our lane wild grapes send out streaming branches ready to seize and grow up you if you should stand talking to the neighbor a minute too long.

Clearly the world has gone mad with June growth and we live in the midst of it all and feel it as abundance on all sides—abundance, and a sense of plenty to be translated into other areas of our lives.

Who can feel any lack while walking through a June meadow where hundreds of daisies are unfolding fresh starched petals, honeysuckle is tossing thousands of honey colored blossoms over the walls, and red clover filling the air with scent.

There is a kind of magic in a stand of delicate fleur-de-lis blue as the sky above. There is magic in drifts of milfoil white as the soft June clouds that drift overhead, and in buttercups everywhere gold as sunshine.

There's magic too in the independence of wild flowers. They bloom whether or not anyone is there to see them, and give out their scent whether or not anyone is at hand to smell them. They reappear year after year without the aid of man.

No one plants or tends these blossoms yet they thrive by the dozen here, by the thousand there, and return annually to the spot they have chosen. When conditions please, they multiply, and even where conditions are not ideal they often grow, a few scattered plants here or there. There is a determination as well as independence in these flowers. They need no coddling, they need no watering, they accept the rain as it comes, they adjust to drought in the dry years. And if conditions are too difficult they scatter their seeds on the wind and spring to life in more favorable areas. Sometimes birds carry the seeds to new spots. And sometimes you and I do as we move through the fields with burs sticking to our clothing.

I've often wondered exactly what a "wild flower" is. Isn't every flower wild somewhere? Bluebonnets carpet the plains of Texas, golden lupin the California coastline below Carmel, and low-growing iris cling to steep banks in the mountains of North Carolina. Probably a wild flower could be called any flower native to the region.

The names they bear are gay, intriguing, romantic, and occasionally even ominous!

Bouncing Bet, hop clover, and mocassin flower conjure up cheery and amusing pictures. Blue curls, star grass, Queen Anne's lace, each as charming as its name, carry you into a dreamy romantic mood. But you are soon brought back to earth by bastard pennyroyal, viper's bugloss (a lovely blue flower), and boneset. How did these ever get their titles?

Once wild flowers have caught your fancy you find yourself stopping at all odd times and places to investigate. Every roadside area yields a wealth of treasure. A daisy field is no longer just a daisy field, or a mountainside a mountainside, but each becomes an invitation to stop and explore.

Wild flowers are not only to enjoy, and to learn about, but some even to eat as well! In the days of my youth our Irish Delia made blancmange out of Irish moss, and shook ripe elderberries into the griddlecake batter. Our ancestors knew more about these things than we. My grandmother used to make a pungent tea with a meadow fragrance from common red clover. Another delicious tea she brewed of maple sap as it comes from the tree. You boil the sap about a half hour, then use it instead of water for making regular tea, or peppermint tea from your own fresh or dried mint leaves. You'll not need to sweeten either variety. In gathering wild plants for foods, be sure to select those in areas free from sprays or fertilizers or roadway dust.

Country people used to tell tales of the gods and the flowers and the peoples of long ago. Some of these legends come down to enchant us today, and to weave an added aura around these flowers of the wilderness. When we drove west a few years ago and came upon the great sunflowers along the highways it was interesting to be told that the Prairie Indians used to enjoy the seeds as food, even as we and our local birds do today. It was also an Indian ritual to place bowls of these seeds on the graves of the dead to nourish the departed spirits on their long journey to the Happy Hunting Ground.

Our familiar red clover was an old-time symbol of good and evil. A five-leaved clover was unlucky, but the four-leaved clover has always been considered a good luck charm. Each leaf has its own significance. They stand for health, wealth, fame, and the last is love! I don't know why the fifth leaf ruins the scheme of things, but it does, so while you are pressing any four-leaved clovers toss away the fives!

Do you know how the cornflower gots its botanical name? A Greek youth named Cyanus was found dead in a field of cornflowers. Since he had been gathering the lovely blossoms for the goddess of flowers, Chloris, she, in gratitude, transformed him into one of the blue flowers and gave it his name Cyanus.

The daisy is named from the Anglo-Saxon "daeges eage" —day's eye because the flower often closes its petals after dark or on cloudy or rainy days.

The Scotch thistle legend is one of my favorites. Once, long years ago in Scotland when the water ran low an army of

Norsemen filled the moat surrounding their stronghold with thistles. The enemy creeping up in the night took off their shoes to wade across the moat. Their agonized screams roused the sleeping Norsemen who quickly eliminated the invaders. Commemorating this victory the thistle became the flower emblem of Scotland.

An explorer in us all enjoys discovering something new and different about plants, their histories, and background. The gardener in us delights in finding and learning about new flower varieties. I like delving into the lore and legends of these wildlings—as well as eating them for dinner! I'll have to confess that Bob takes a somewhat dim view of any meadow greens I present him with. I tell him he really must be experimental, and he asks, succinctly,

"Why?"

June is the month when it is especially pleasant to arrange flowers in the house. All of a sudden we have all the blooms we can possibly pick—and such a variety. Even the bathrooms get their share. Here I fill tiny Mexican vases with all colors of pansies.

Pick a rosebud and set it in a vase. Each day it fills out, grows larger, and the color alters slightly. Gradually the petals unfold until they are full blown. Every hour from the moment you cut it until it fades this rose looks slightly different. The constant change is fascinating to observe. Arrange any flowers from the garden or the florist and the same thing occurs. From day to day every blossom changes a little. The petals of certain varieties grow larger, such as those of zinnias, snapdragons, roses, delphiniums, and shasta daisies.

The constant change is but a part of the fun of live blooms in the house. You also fill your rooms with fragrance and color, and, best of all, you bring these blossoms close by for a keener appreciation. A bouquet imparts a particular kind of vitality to the corner where it stands. The room comes alive in a new way. You feel a little gayer, a little happier, and you don't quite know why.

Each summer month has its moods and manners. Flower bouquets reflect these. Iris and peonies breathe of June. All the bright annuals, zinnias, marigolds, cornflowers and snapdragons suggest summer at its height. Dahlias and chrysanthemums are the spirit of autumn.

In making bouquets I fear I break all the rules and purely have fun. I have no special containers and absolutely no knowledge of the intricate art of flower arranging. From a lovely antique Chinese vase to a rustic wicker basket with a cooking pan of water inside, my choice of containers is infinite. Jam jars, sugar bowls, baking dishes, as well as a little green glass vase that we watched blown in Williamsburg, Virginia. All these and more offer themselves as possibilities. Let no rules inhibit you either. At any and every season choose the varieties you especially admire, the container you'd like to use, and arrange the blooms in ways that especially appeal. This makes flower arranging effortless, free, and pure joy.

Garden flowers abound in lore and legend, in old-time tales, and they also have their place in history. One of my favorite tales is an enchanting legend about the peony, a story from China, for it is in the Orient that this lovely flower had its beginnings. A Chinese gentleman had two treasures, a little three-year-old daughter named Quince Bud, and a single, rare, black peony flower that he had developed. One day the small child was playing in the garden where the blossom stood. Her nurse left her for a moment and, too young to understand, she picked her father's prize black peony. A passing lord on horseback saw the child holding the bloom and coveted it for his white marble palace. When Quince Bud would not part with the flower, he angrily kidnapped both small child and blossom and galloped off. The terrified youngster clutched the peony squeezing it in her tiny hands until the petals dropped one by one. When the frantic father discovered the loss of his beloved daughter, the neighbors pointed out a trail of black petals clearly visible on the road. Small Quince Bud was brought tearfully and happily home. And next year the plant produced not just one but an armful of great black peonies.

The iris is also an old, old flower. Iris are recognizably represented on the walls of the Temple of Karnak which was raised in about 1000 B.C. Louis VII of France adopted this flower as his blazon during the Crusades. It was subsequently named after him, the Fleur-de-Louis, later shortened to Fleur-de-Lis. This blossom is also called the flower of chivalry because it has a sword for a leaf and a lily at its heart. Look into the next iris you see for the lily shape visible at the center. In old Dutch paintings of the life of Christ, you often see an iris painted in somewhere to symbolize his royal descent. And just to come back to practicalities, in ancient days in Great Britain, the Highlanders used to make ink out of iris roots!

As you delve into old books what delightful items you discover. For example, delphinium are grown from Tibet to California and just about everywhere in between. In parts of Siberia this blossom grows wild. The name larkspur was originally lark's heel, and if you can get this near a lark, you can imagine that the buds resemble his "heel."

Mrs. Glover, who can kill a copperhead with a rake and never a second thought, runs for the house and pulls down the shades in a thunderstorm.

I don't believe I could possibly kill a copperhead with a rake because when I see one I find myself instinctively moving so rapidly in the opposite direction that before I could even wield the rake I am far away in the next lot. But thunderstorms I happen to like.

I was home alone all afternoon of the first thunderstorm of the season. I could feel the forces gather in the strong hot wind that bent the meadow grass and turned the maples in their new summer dress to tossing bright green plumes. I marveled at the give there is in a maple tree and its branches.

The meadow grass, too, was host to the wind that rippled over, shading it silver here and dark, shiny green there. Any door left open for an instant slammed. And now and then the dust from the gravel drive took off in a swirl. It was clear and sunny but the ominous wind let me know something was stirring—something was definitely going to happen.

As the afternoon passed a heat and tension gathered in the air. By five the sky in the north had turned blue-black, and about suppertime the sun disappeared. Bob was away at a meeting until late evening so I was alone with the storm. Great gray-blue thunderheads moved over the northern sky while at the south the heavens were an arc of yellow-orange merging with the gray.

Thunder began, gently at first, and started in the north, then on every side, subtle, loud, in great rolling cadences. The sky grew blacker and blacker, the yellow arc disappeared. The wind ceased altogether and stillness hung in the air.

On the brick terrace a few huge drops fell, then more, until they merged. The rain came harder and louder. Presently the terrace was a lake, each drop splashing as it fell. A gray mist enveloped Pop's Mountain. The splash of water pouring from the heavens drowned out all other sounds, and a rich warm smell of growth rose from the land.

At first the lightning was a yellow glow here and there around the horizon and then jagged streaks pierced the blackened sky and angled towards earth—bringing nitrogen, they say.

The rain barrel, nearly empty this morning, was now overflowing. The brook roared, there was a freshness in the air, and I felt a kind of exhilaration. Crashing sounds filled the heavens as thunder tossed among the clouds. Broken twigs scattered across the lawn, and yard-long branches cracked off and brushed over the grass to settle on its new bright green.

In a few minutes the wave of water passed over and the noise of wind and falling drops gradually quieted. The air was fresh and cool and all the garden everywhere was a rich, shining, wet green. The thunder faded, the lightning diminished to an occasional glow over the hills. Tree trunks were purple-black and the leaves in this half hour surely had grown inches. They hung like heavy dripping curtains. In this single shower we had lost our neighbors. We see these neighbors' houses in winter and gradually, as the leaves open, they disappear. We could glimpse all of them this morning, but not tonight. Now I am alone in a world of green, a world of growth, where no other house is visible.

Bob would be late so when it grew dark I went to bed on the porch. I could hear the water dripping in the surrounding maples, watch the fireflies dance treetop high, and then came the sound of the whippoorwill—"*Time*-for-*sleep—time*-for-*sleep—time*-for-*sleep*—."

There was almost a sigh over the land as it gratefully soaked up the shower. Thunder, rain, and wind had ceased. You could sense deep-down roots everywhere stretching out in new growth.

Everybody sleeps, and almost everybody who doesn't live in the midst of a city has a porch and yet how few people put the two together and sleep on the porch. There are positively no words to describe the experience of sleeping out in summer. We move onto our sleeping porch in May and move in in late September. For four months we enjoy nights there, and sleeping becomes something quite different. The birds singing at dawn are the features of May. This can drive our city friends mad but we happen to like it. Now in June it is fireflies as you drift off, the urbanites perfer these. Later come the comfortable and secure sounds of summer insects, the cicadas, the katydids, the crickets. We are there when the moon makes fabulous patterns out of the chair shadows, when the rain dances on the roof, and when stars are bright and close.

During any month myriads of outdoor scents invade the porch. Dianthus and roses mingle their fragrances on June nights. In July it is the lily, and all summer we smell the meadow scents. With all these attractions it begins to sound as if we spend the night listening and smelling and never sleep at all. But we do sleep and soundly. The various pleasures hover around the rim of consciousness, and in a half dream we appreciate them. Waking in the morning freshness to the sound of the brook is the final touch, and a magnificent way of starting the day. I am sure if people in high places who have great responsibilities could sleep surrounded by all the gentle country night sounds they would find great easement, and would discharge their responsibilities and make wise decisions with greater inner calm. It is almost impossible to go to sleep on a porch in summer and not wake refreshed and really made over.

Occasionally, though, winter or summer we all have times when sleep is elusive. When I move rapidly through too many daytime activities and maintain the rush too long, the momentum tends to take over. At night I keep right on moving mentally and lie awake a long time. How desirable is a proper balance between motion and rest, and how difficult it is at times for us to achieve it. Alternation lies everywhere in nature. Even cows and chickens take time off from producing milk and eggs. Only we human beings foolishly forget these solid well-known truths at times and try to live our lives from crest of wave to crest of wave with never a trough between. We forget that in the trough the next crest builds.

A rainy June day leads me to bills and budget. I used to not like the budget, and could never add a column of figures and come out the same way twice. But now the budget is a joy. Perhaps because it is a kind of solid area, a realm with definite boundaries in a world of indefinites.

I flee from the budget into life with its beautiful and welcome vagaries, and at times from these very same vagaries I retreat to the certainties of the budget. Here you may be $100 behind or $100 ahead, but at least it is definite, there before you on paper. My hazy nature is so full of vagaries that it really needs some boundaries and the budget proves one good one.

The saddest words of tongue or pen to me are, "We can't afford it." I say it differently. "We can afford *anything if* we are willing to pay the price." In the budget *anything* is possible—just anything at all! If we want to go to Switzerland, Siam, or Seattle, and if we set aside x number of dollars for x numbers of months or weeks, we will eventually have the needed funds in hand. Of course, we could just take all the money in the bank at the moment and go. But if we did this we might have to stop eating for several months, paying insurance, income tax, and perhaps go to jail.

In our budget we have a trip fund, and into this goes a certain sum regularly and any surplus. And first thing we know there is a trip waiting. It may be a short nearby one, or a long far-off one—but a trip. In the pages of this budget book everything has its order and place. The income tax gets saved all year so paying it is never a blow. We set aside regularly for all overhead so the money is waiting when needed.

Of course, this sounds neat and pat, and yet terrible errors occur. Our budget is a source of both agony and ecstasy. It is a challenge, but I couldn't do without it.

Some people are just naturally bright about money and probably don't need a budget. They go along and come out right. I believe Bob would be this way. In spite of my Scotch ancestry, I find money can slip away from me in a most amazing manner. But with the budget, it doesn't.

Bob did a masterly job in setting it up and he does the basic figuring and adjusting, if needed. I do the monthly adding. His week-ends and evenings are short enough and if I can help by doing any secretarial work, I am pleased to.

To put it simply, if you can put a budget simply, ours works like this: There is the checkbook which is always right, of course, and the budget book which we always hope will be right. Our budget inhabits a ledger divided by pages and into sections. First comes income, then taxes, insurance, telephone, medical, food, clothes, Bob's cash, my cash, etc. We have about twenty categories AND a cushion, vacation fund, savings. Under each heading a certain regular sum is entered on the first day of each month. Monthly expenses as they occur are entered on the proper pages. Then bills are paid and surplus and deficits noted. The last day of the month all these surpluses are totalled together, deficits subtracted. The sum is then subtracted from income that month. At the end of the month the sum in the budget book should match the sum in the checkbook.

Therein lies the challenge. It is incredible what discrepancies can occur with this simple system which just shows that even as concrete a thing as a budget has its mysteries and vagaries. Once last fall the budget and checkbook for three months running had been at great variance and always, of course, to our loss. We literally had less money in the bank than the budget told us we had. Bob, who can usually unravel my mistakes, this time was nonplussed. At last in desperation he said,

"Why don't you take it to the bank—surely there'll be someone there who would have ideas about household budgets and could help."

"Yes, maybe they'll suggest how to set it up differently and better," I thought. I was losing confidence in our method.

"The bank certainly ought to know about budgets," Bob concluded.

So off I went in awe—Banks are always Right, always Wise, always Bright about figures. I found myself, ledger in hand, explaining our budget and current problems to one of the officers.

He couldn't have been more pleasant and interested. He listened carefully.

"Now," I finished, "I think there is something wrong with our system. I'd like to learn from you and improve on what we are doing. How do you work a household budget?"

"Well, to tell the truth," he laughed, "my wife and I never had one!"

"You didn't," I gasped. "Well, what do other people do—how do they get along—your other depositors?"

"As far as I can figure out our depositors don't have budgets either, they just draw till there's none left, and sometimes overdraw, and then wait for the next salary check!"

This certainly came as a shock.

As he went over our budget, he opined that he had never seen one like it, and that he thought it rather interesting. He couldn't see what was wrong currently or why anything should go wrong.

"If you add right you should have no problem," he concluded closing the book and handing it back. At that moment my awe of banks collapsed, and ever since they have seemed quite human.

So——I thought on the way home——if the bank can't figure our budget, *we've got to.* Taking a deep breath we decided to cancel off all past and current discrepancies, take our cherished surplus for which we had many other plans, alas, and fill in present gaps. We'd bury the past and start fresh. We'd MAKE IT WORK OURSELVES!

Mr. Emerson would have approved of this self-reliant approach.

Together we went over the basic structure, made a few minor changes and started fresh. The bank must have had some effect, be it indirect. Perhaps I gained a confidence, at least in our method, because since then and since I do a mid-month partial check, all is well. Except for a few adding mistakes here and there which Bob or I catch, we seem to come out right.

Some days, some moments we find ourselves lifted above our usual selves. We become more than we are. Thoughts greater than we come blowing through us—everything we do turns out just right. All relationships are rich and rewarding. Everything we touch flourishes. The bread rises, the right telephone calls come in, and the mail brings great things. This is how it is. We feel connected, plugged in, so to say, to some force greater than we that moves through us. But we don't even stop to think of this—we just soar. On such a day by nine in the morning I may have bread in the oven, cookies made, the washing on the line, and the beds changed, and maybe an article I have been thinking about outlined.

Of course we have other days that we move through in an average sort of way without anything special.

On still other days we wake feeling *less* than we are. Our best ideas come to nought. Dull tasks are endless and hours drag. We function quite apart from any power beyond our finite uninspired selves.

Everything we see about us is in a constant state of change and it is not surprising that our moods are too. Perhaps the need is to accept low moments as temporary, just hold on, and know they will pass. Then we can coast patiently along on the level days, accomplishing, for these are the times of lists and of doing this and this. When the high moments come we can let go and soar. Of course I never remember in these peak times to accept their fleeting quality and am often distressed as I thud back to earth. But you cannot live constantly in air. Even a plane must land on firm ground to refuel before the next flight.

June is the month is which you rise high and become more than you are, so it is perhaps also the time to remember the thump of earth on the return trip. Will I ever learn to enjoy the heights, build on them, and when they slip away accept and make use of the level stretches?

Nothing is younger and more vulnerable than a day-old, still damp-from-the-egg chipping sparrow! There is a nest in our rose vine by the vegetable garden. We watched the birds mate, build, lay eggs, and now the eggs are hatched. Each evening after supper we go out to inspect. The book says that in ten days they will be full grown. It is incredible to realize that anything so new-looking and helpless can be mature in ten days.

Ten days later we go out to see how they have grown. The parent birds hover in a branch overhead, chipping away and, I suppose, communicating something to the youngsters in the nest. We parted the leaves to peek and out flew all four directly at us. We quickly stepped aside and the little birds soared over to the walls and disappeared in the lower tree branches. I don't know whether this was their first flight or whether they had been out before and gone back. It was interesting then to hear the parent birds coaching their children while they gathered them together and headed somewhere for the night.

Part of the fun of June is all the new birds flying off to lives of their own and leaving the nests. The phoebes under the eaves of the shop look as if they were ready to leave at any moment and the robins in the maple by the terrace have gone.

The music that wakes us every morning is composed of myriads of bird songs all blended together into a melody that starts the day in a wonderful vein. You hear a lot about bird songs in the morning, but at dusk the music is equally melodious. These are the evenings when we sit on the porch and listen to the thrush and the catbird and the rose-breasted grosbeak. All those who have greeted the day now help draw it to a close.

Sunny June day follows sunny June day. The trees are full out and fresh green. The meadow is flower filled and gardens everywhere are bursting out with blossoms and vegetables. A kind of serenity flows over the landscape towards the end of the month, and we feel it too. It is no longer a great occasion to eat our asparagus, and spinach, and lettuce, and beets, and onions, and carrots, but just the accepted thing. We are surrounded by flowers to pick and vegetables to harvest. The vegetables are all under their clean and bouncy hay mulch so pleasant to walk on.

We think and plan for the beach, for picnics, for week-end guests, for all that a summer in the country brings. While the long twilight gradually fades into night myriads of fireflies sparkle over our meadow. There is magic in these tiny creatures and seeing them fills your spirit with gaiety. When we have friends for dinner we sit outside and watch the darkness fall, and the fireflies light it with their nightly dance. On the brook terrace the orchids set out last month are sending up new shoots and flower buds. Nearby the hammock gently moving in the breeze issues its almost irresistible invitation—"Come for a lazy hour and bring a book—or just come."

PART 3

Season of relaxing and savoring the fruits

THE SAP HAS REACHED the topmost branch. The great push of burgeoning new growth slows its pace. The drive of spring planting in which we took part so eagerly has gradually diminished. A natural momentum carries on while we stand back and view the fruits of our earlier labors. We look, we wonder, we respect these forces at work over the landscape.

All that we have initiated in our gardens the last few months rolls along pretty much on its own now. Our participation is less urgently needed and our personal hurry slackens. Things are what they are for better or worse. Too late for different plans for this year, too early for next, so we accept what is and find it basically good. Living totally in the now as nature fulfills herself around us, we savor the best and discover fresh rewards each day. Time itself seems almost to pause during these weeks as we revel in plentiful fruits, vegetables and flowers. These are our days for appreciating.

How easily we slide into this relaxing interlude of carefree ways. The weather warms, the sun shines down. We grow dreamy with vacationing, picnics, drowsing in the hammock, breakfast on the beach, while the spirit of leisure and informal living seeps into our bones and hearts.

7

July is sand and sea and warm blue days

JULY IS THE SEASON of beaches and a blue sea, and an azure sky with white sails along the horizon. These are the days of dinner on the terrace, the sun-warmed scent of ripe huckleberries in high pastures and blue chicory flowering along the railroad tracks. In our meadow bright orange butterfly weed is host to a hundred brown butterflies each morning and black-eyed Susans sweep through the grass. Day lilies bloom in profusion along the stone walls and the brook terrace. Up the gorge where we sometimes walk in the cool of evening, linden trees are fringed with pendent clusters of waxy white flowers whose haunting fragrance follows you all the way along. Here and there in the still, rock-bound pools of the Saugatuck River an interesting golden-green scum folds great scallops over the black surface.

At night a variety of insects crowd the screen and certain little characters wiggle through the mesh to their doom. Alas, if they weren't so avid for the light they'd live longer! After supper we often wander down the meadow on a tour of discovery. Here in the bog we find water hemlock—a wild flower with a leaf like a columbine and blossoms like snowflakes. The field grass is tipped reddish and stretches of yellow butter-and-eggs lead the eye over the rolling contours.

July is the month of colors—with red, white and blue heading the list. Red is for the scarlet tanager, flashing over the fields, for geraniums, for the first tomatoes, for hollyhocks, and for little children in red bathing suits wading along the shore. White is for daisies, milfoil, Queen Anne's lace, and whitecaps on a windy sea. Blue is for the delphiniums, the platycodon, the inky dark lobelia, and the sea and sky.

July is all the madly brilliant annuals, too. Orange and scarlet zinnias, tawny marigolds, petunias in every shade and feathery lavender cosmos. Our first garden cucumbers embellish the salad. Standing on the sweet-smelling hay mulch we pick and taste the earliest ripening tomatoes, juicy and warm from the sun. The first golden corn comes steaming to the table and we eat countless ears dripping with melted butter and Sea Salt. July is summer stretching out—rich, vigorous, going places, and reaching in all directions.

One fabulous sparkling morning all plans must be shelved for a whole long day on the beach. Off I went with yogurt, peaches and plums, *Sixpence In Your Shoe* by Phyllis McGinley, and the little pillow I am embroidering. The pillow is made of old neckties, snips of bright-colored velvet, and some samples of Fortuny prints that my sister Connie gave me. I have already made four of these ten inch square pillows. This is number five. I pin a design of patchwork on one side, baste the pieces together and do fancy embroidery where they join. This all makes a pleasant summer pastime, and, when finished, becomes an enchanting gift.

After a long lazy day on the sand with the salt air and blue waves, reading, swimming and sewing, and watching children build castles down by the water's edge, I feel as if I had been far, far away when I turn in the drive in the late afternoon. This is such a deliciously free and lovely time of year. So few clothes, so few deadlines, so few commitments of any kind. It is truly a month of freedom.

Even the birds, so earnestly filled with householding and launching new families last month, now gather nonchalantly on the light wires—there may be seven or thirteen together. No longer do they fly in pairs, but in small flocks dart here and swoop there with carefree air and no pressing purpose. Perhaps it is a holiday time for them too. We no longer hear the rich melodious early morning symphonies of last month, but instead casual, intermittent music rings forth at any time of day, just as we, when filled with the joy of the moment, spontaneously whistle a gay little tune, or break into song.

This is the month to celebrate freedom officially with the magic of sparklers, pinwheels and showers of man-made stars. Freedom is a thought-provoking word, a vital element in the personal living of all of us.

But is anyone ever totally free? Would you want to be? I would not. Some of the richest moments come from relinquishing some of my freedom to family, community, housekeeping and work responsibilities—yes, even meeting deadlines, much as I sputter about them at times.

If we take no part in what goes on around us and have few or no responsibilities, if we have no one to be concerned for, we may be free in a way but at what cost in fulfillment? "To hope and fear for someone else is the only thing that gives a man complete sense of his own existence," writes Alexander Dumas.

Within any certain pattern of living each of us is free to make decisions, to change directions. No matter what our outer conditions and commitments, we are still completely free to alter our thinking about them. This particular change can often lead to a change in these outward circumstances. Perhaps this is the most challenging freedom of all—freedom of thought and its consequences.

One day I was sitting on the terrace sipping grape juice, looking at our eighteen rose bushes and thinking about Cleopatra. She obviously had more than eighteen when she spread a carpet of petals a foot and a half deep for Mark Antony. I am content with our number, however. They give us ample flowers all season and are easy to tend. Cleopatra, I remind myself, had hundreds of slaves! Many roses are in full flower now and a number more in bud. The plants are healthy, bug and disease free, and no spray is needed. The whole effect is entirely pleasing. I never can decide whether I like roses better in bud or in a full-blown state. I know I enjoy watching them drop their petals on the ground, a few at a time spilling over the mulch and turning the rich brown cocoa hulls to a changing pattern of bright color.

This particular afternoon was one of those idyllic times when anything can happen. For several weeks our light blue delphinium in the perennial bed near the roses has been in full bloom. It is almost like a bush with sprays of side buds opening freshly each morning. It had been the center of interest for the local hummingbirds who come several times a day to sip nectar. Now today one little creature appeared, darting and hovering first here and then there. We rarely see these birds come or go, so fast are they on the wing, they are either there or gone. Presently a most remarkable thing happened. The tiny bird rose in the air, perhaps ten feet high and a little to one side of the perennial bed. Flying so fast I could hardly follow him with my eye, he described an arc whose central low point was the delphinium itself. Here he swung back and forth like a pendulum in a great semi-circle. He did this about ten times and then took off. I was fascinated by his performance, and by the brief glimpse into one of the many other worlds that interpenetrate ours. When it was over I rushed to the bird book and found that this is what hummingbirds do. The lady is always somewhere near the lowest part of the arc —next time I must look for her. It's a kind of courting dance although it seems a little late for courting now.

While looking up hummingbirds I discovered some other interesting facts about them. It seems that they are the only birds that can fly backwards as well as forwards. Though tiny, they have great strength and never hesitate to attack and do battle with a larger bird when the occasion demands it. They migrate from Hudson Bay to Panama and pass over six hundred miles of open sea. Their nests are lined with fern down and milkweed all woven together with a spider's web. Into this soft, cozy cradle eggs no larger than white beans are laid.

I stand in the vegetable garden about five o'clock in the afternoon wondering what to have for dinner. Will it be onions, purple-topped turnips, squash, beets, spinach, snow peas, string beans, a choice of three kinds of lettuce, and perhaps our rhubarb steamed for dessert (with a bit of sour cream on top)? All the vegetables, fresh and crisp, wait in the earth for my decision. Whatever we don't have tonight we shall have tomorrow and tomorrow and over the week-end. It is so much more interesting to stand in the garden deciding what to have than to pick it out in the supermarket, pleasant as that can be. We have more of everything in the vegetable garden than we can possibly eat. This makes it a joy to share produce with almost everyone who comes to the house and, of course, bit by bit I am filling the freezer. I pick a little more than we can eat for dinner each night and freeze the surplus. Thus the freezer fills gradually and effortlessly. It is a very contented and thrifty sensation to be tucking food aside to enjoy during the winter months.

Some July days are just plain hot—the air presses in and down upon you and you seem unable to move fast. The way to get along with these days I find is not to move fast. Quite a lot gets done in a slower tempo. One time in July we drove across the western plains and the Mojave Desert. The dry heat was something to cope with. We ended up soaking washcloths and bath towels with water and driving with them on our heads! While dramatic in a way, it was an experience I would just as soon not repeat! At that time I promised myself I would never let New England humidity bother me again. I would take it as the slowdown nature surely means it to be. And this is how it has worked out. When I stick to my desk as I write, or to the chair at dinner, I remember that desert and feel better about it!

These weeks we seldom have quite enough rain for the garden so we water. The season is unusually dry and we can only hope no serious drought lies ahead. It is interesting being a lifeline to the plants in this way. The colors of flowers grow lighter when roots are not getting adequate moisture. Our Garden Party rose whose white petals are tinted pink, remains pure white when the plant is too dry. If I soak the roots in the morning by afternoon the petals are pink-rimmed again. The magenta milfoil fades to pale pink, and also, with watering, comes back in a few hours. We have a deep well, but only 3 gallons a minute so we must be thrifty. Running water from the hose around the base of each plant uses less water than the sprinkler. The rain barrel at one end of the terrace is a big help. These are the days when we especially appreciate having only a small number of cultivated flowers. Two beds 6 x 12 are fairly easy to water when the need arises.

It's all very well as a gardener to relate closely to nature and nature's ways, but it also has a slight drawback. When rain is needed I feel sort of parched, too. Of course, on the other hand, when rain does come, we gardeners have a tremendous sense of joy and relief, and can almost feel the earth absorbing water and roots replenishing themselves.

What a little thing it takes to start the day on the right

note. I was squeezing orange juice this morning when a cardinal lit on the clothesline outside the kitchen window and the early sun shone on his brilliant plumage. That simple and sparkling touch of beauty set the day off to a fine start. It was a special day anyway because Jeff was coming for a visit.

Where is our grandson? I am waiting on the station platform for this young thirteen-year-old who will be carrying a suitcase and I don't see him. Other people get off, but no Jeff. There is a boy down the platform—or is it a boy—it seems more like a thatched roof moving along. And now before I can think further, this thatched roof moves upon me.

"Hi, Grandma, here I am."

"Why, Jeff," I gasp. "Hello, how good to see you."

I gasp because here we have the Beatles incarnate. I have no war with these young Englishmen beyond what they have done to the hairdos of America. I protest this when I see handsome girls in their teens whose attractive foreheads and eyes are almost completely hidden under a mop of uncombed hair. I wonder about the color of their eyes. Youths used to dream of the eyes of their best girls—but now how can they see them? And the boys are just as bad with their floor mops.

To think that our beloved grandson has succumbed to this rage! After recovering from my first shock I took one of Jeff's bundles and we headed for the car. My face must have been an open book because presently he said, "What's the matter, Grandma?"

"Well, nothing exactly, Jeff, but let's go and get a haircut on the way home."

"But Grandma, I had it cut not long ago."

"I know, but let's get another."

"I don't really think I need it."

"I'll tell you how it is, Jeff. You can wear it as long as you like all the rest of the summer, but the week you are here I am adamant. No Beatles."

"Aw, Grandma."

"I simply can't talk to you if I can't see your eyes, to say nothing of what it's doing to your sight, and I expect that we may have things to say to each other in these next days."

"All right, Grandma—but just a trim."

"No, not even a trim, but a real haircut and all that top off—I do insist."

"Maybe it is a little long," and a sort of shy, half smile flickered around the corners of his mouth.

Surely I must get off all this hair before his grandfather sees him, or anyone, for that matter. He looked like a tired sheepdog.

"What are we going to do this week, Grandma?" Jeff asked gaily as we walked toward the barber.

"Oh, we'll swim, picnic, play badminton and go visiting maybe."

"Great—and can we go to the movies?"

"Probably we'll do just that, too."

During his April visit we were in a great state of rapport, and now I could feel it return as we wandered cheerily down Main Street and he began telling me he was learning to play tennis, and had been camping in a tent in a field with a friend. It's wonderful to feel this warm, sharing affection and closeness and responsiveness in Jeff.

We entered the barber shop.

"This young man needs a haircut," I said firmly. The barber smiled compassionately at me.

"I think you can take it all off," I said as Jeff climbed up into the chair and the man tied the towel around him.

Jeff looked up at the barber beside him and with great dignity and in a voice a couple years older said, "Just a trim, please." The barber smiled, their eyes met, and they were at one in a masculine world far beyond the territory of grandmothers. For the moment they were two men understanding each other, and I was not there.

I went to get my films next door with a pang of loneliness for the small boy Jeff had been. Now we had no tractable child but a teenager—a mercurial, volatile, vulnerable young person with his own ideas and preferences and one who no longer accepts that his parents and grandparents are always right. Painful as it can be there is rightness in all of this—the rightness of one season giving way to the next. One phase of growth ending, another beginning.

When I picked Jeff up a half hour later he looked neat and trim, the barber had effected a beautiful compromise.

"There, that's great," I said. "You have a forehead again and I can see your eyes." He seemed quite pleased with the result himself.

"Can we go for a swim right away?" Jeff asked gaily as we got in the car.

"I don't know why not."

"I can change in the car, can't I, Grandma, and you have your suit on under, haven't you?"

Now we are in rapport again—but isn't Jeff sitting a little taller, a little straighter?

July is the month of summer visits. My sister Connie came up for a few days and while we were standing outside watering the garden, she began telling me about all her recent peace activities.

It is difficult for me to consider peace on a vast scale with any specific thoughts about what can be done. But if I can bring peace down to an individual matter between myself and another, I can perhaps get some understanding of the subject.

Suppose you are in disagreement with someone about something of importance to you or the other person, and it has thrown you, for the moment, out of harmony with him. Perhaps you are both quite heated on the subject. Here is an interesting procedure to follow, and one that produces amazing results. First you make up your mind that your opinions are not on the agenda for the moment, and that *no matter what,* you are *not* going to express them. This seems practically impossible but can be achieved with a great and worthwhile effort. Next you tell the other person that you are in disagreement with him. You are not going to express your point of view but would like instead to know better and try to understand his.

Now the fun begins, because the other person pours forth, as fast as he can get the words out, his opinions, fully expecting to be interrupted. And you have a terrible time not breaking in because, of course, he is obviously so wrong! But if you can persist, something very strange and almost miraculous occurs. Since you have made up your mind that you are not going to express your own ideas you've been listening in a different way. Instead of waiting impatiently for a break in the flow of words for you to insert contradictions, you find yourself actually *listening* to what the other person is saying. Through his words you come to an awareness of how he inwardly feels—something you never knew when you were so concerned in expressing exactly how you felt.

The other strange thing that happens is that when the other person finds you listening in this new way and becomes aware that you really are not going to interrupt, he slows up, lowers his voice, stops exaggerating, and, in fact, may even backtrack a little and hesitate to express some views about which a few moments before he was adamant.

Your real effort to learn about and understand his way of thinking opens him to your ideas. Earlier antagonisms between you both disappear and a great sense of peace prevails.

July is the month of vacations and trips to far and near places. The slices of conversation you overhear in stores and on the street deal, for the most part, with comings and goings, mountains and seashore, Europe and camping, and every mail brings postal cards from the Adirondacks, from Greece, California and Switzerland.

Both Bob and I have very active wanderlusts. We like to go anywhere at any time. On a moment's notice I will pack my suitcase for any destination. When we are going on a trip I literally do pack a week or two ahead and then, of course, I have to keep taking out things like my hairbrush and a belt and shoes. I often forget to put these back at the last moment so when I get there I am missing needed articles. Bob, on the other hand, packs the night before and consequently forgets a few things from not thinking ahead. We each follow our own path and are forgetful in our own personal ways, and yet come out with the same results!

When our children went to California to college, we found ourselves going often to the Coast and camping on the way. I believe a little of the gypsy dwells in us all, and once wakened, can readily take over. We started off with a small green tent to which we became very attached and have used ever since.

This tent is translucent, and early morning sunlight turns the interior to a wonder of golden green. At night the moon sends shadows darting across its sloping walls—shadows to watch as you fall asleep. Rain patters on the canvas with an intimate cozy sound.

One time outside Bryce Canyon we were wakened at the break of day by a flock of thousands of sheep undulating towards us. There was no time to think or be afraid. In an instant they were upon us. As though our tent were a mere clump of bushes they parted and flowed around it, guided by three horsemen who brought up the rear. With happy relief we greeted the mountain shepherds and went back to sleep.

Nor will I forget waking in a mountain canyon, looking out the tent flap and seeing, five feet from our heads, an immense moose breathing down upon us. In the Arches National Monument we were wakened by huge beetles silhouetted in the moonlight, crawling up one side of the tent and sliding scratchily down the other. Beetles follow their accustomed trail, it seems, willy nilly. One day a truck load of sweet corn bound for market travelled the highway ahead of us. Every now and then an ear or two bounced off. How good they were boiled and buttered for dinner that night on our little Coleman stove!

On the sandy shore of a Minnesota lake, a small boy appeared at dusk each day with a net of Northern pike. He and his father had caught more than they could eat. Would we like some? Such is the sharing way of campers.

You'll never be lonely camping. What a warm and cordial lot are those who like the outdoor life. I often wonder if camping makes us all more friendly and sharing, and ready to speak to our neighbor and help him, or do people with these traits like camping?

Living in the open your walls are the tall steeple-shaped spruce, the lodgepole pine; your roof is the blue sky by day and the starry heavens by night. In the morning you feel the warmth of the rising sun and in the late afternoon the coming coolness of night.

Something else rather wonderful happens when you camp. You discover a particular joy in the ordinary acts of daily living—washing clothes, cooking, sleeping, bathing. Because you are in no hurry you give these common tasks your full attention, your complete awareness, and there comes a kind of magic into them.

Standing on the firm solid earth before the little gas stove, under the tarpaulin Bob has stretched, I breathe in the tantalizing odor of steak and cooking vegetables. You are always so hungry outdoors that cooking is a special pleasure. It presents amusing challenges quite different from those at home. Will the pine pollen fall into the salad I have just made? How would it taste? Has it perhaps some special vitamins? The fresh-gathered raspberries for dessert seem flavored with the high meadows where we found them this afternoon. And if we are not alert the brown squirrel will dart over and steal a few. Incidentally, when cooking out there are no crumb problems, and the squirrel and chipmunk with whom you share them become your fast friends.

When we sleep in our little tent the stars at night are close. Each breath of air pure and fresh is spiced with a smoky scent of dying fires. When you waken you are extremely close to the newness of a fresh day at its beginning.

Camping develops your ability to adapt, and adapt, and to

adapt to adapting. You become at home in strange places among strange people. But, of course, what happens is that nothing and no one is strange any more. You really care about your neighbor camper whom you never saw before today and may never see again after tomorrow. And you learn he cares about you. In your closeness to nature you find closeness to your fellow man too. Or maybe when living in the woods you have more time to think about such things.

In July everybody you telephone is somewhere else—either on the beach or on vacation, and half the time you're somewhere else too. Your friends moan that they have been trying to reach you by phone all week. This is the month that a beautiful leisure descends upon the days. I look at the books in the bookcase which I have been promising myself all winter I would read, and now I read them. A book which I took off the shelf a few days ago is called *Rose Recipes,* by Jean Gordon. Whether you are given to eating roses or not, it makes fascinating reading. It seems that in Turkey they have rose syrup on the table just as we have salt and toss a dash into practically everything. You can make roses into jam, conserves, frostings, pancakes, and soup, to list but a few.

Last month each rose that bloomed roused in me such tender feelings that I couldn't have thought of eating them but this month we have so many that I might be able to.

Almost everything in the book called for rose water or rose syrup. Between the two you can make all recipes and also a glamorous eyewash or skin lotion. It was obvious I couldn't get anywhere with the cooking recipes unless I had a jar of rose syrup on hand. In the Egyptian Embassy, or maybe the Greek one, they made rose syrup by wrapping a lot of rose petals in soft white material after sunning them, shading them, drying them and airing them and a number of other processes for weeks. Next they boiled them in a teakettle of water, attaching a rubber hose to the spout. The hose was run through a pan of cold water and allowed to drip the condensed steam into a bowl on the floor. This, the book said, was simple. Maybe so, but it made me feel we should keep the roses for arrangements! Certainly if I were going to ease roses into our menu I mustn't begin by having Bob fall over rubber hoses when he came home at night.

Other recipes involved filter cloths, drying racks of screening, and great complications. They obviously originated in the days of hundreds of slaves. After a delightful afternoon in the hammock with the book, I picked four huge red roses, fully out. (Our roses had been sprayed only once, way back in May.) I took off the petals and cut off the slightly bitter-tasting base of each. These four roses I simmered, covered, for about a half hour in a small amount of water and a half cup of brown sugar. Strained, it made 1 1/3 tall glasses of fluid that looked like wine and tasted the way roses smell.

My method was so easy I wondered if it would work. Looking through the book I came to Shrewsbury cakes. We were going to the Shakespeare Theatre in a few days with a friend. I said I'd bring the picnic, and surely this old English recipe with roses in it would be appropriate. The cakes came out like crisp little sugar cookies with golden brown rims and tasted wonderful. I went on to rose custard and even basted the broiled chicken for dinner that night with the remaining syrup. I never realized before that roses were such a source of flavor. The cookies were delicious—the custard, too, and the chicken had an exotic taste.

This seems to be the month to experiment, so I next decided to cook day lilies. They were blooming rampantly all along Valley Forge Road and I thought Nature could part with a few. Inbred in us all is a slight fear of eating roadside plants, perhaps due to the uncertainty of mushrooms, so taking my courage in hand, I set forth with a basket. I would try the blossoms for lunch and see how they came out, and how *I* came out before offering them for dinner. The blossoms and buds looked pretty in the basket and equally handsome in the pot after I had washed them and carefully removed a few stray bees. It took only about five minutes to boil them. With butter and salt they *were* heavenly with a flavor as subtle as an artichoke and equally delectable. The only disappointment was they weren't as beautiful cooked as when they first went in the pot. I kept taking note all afternoon of how I felt—no bad effects.

When I told Bob that I was all set to cook day lilies some night soon for dinner, he gave me one of those looks that a husband gives a wife when she suggests eating day lilies!

Next on my list of experiments is squash blossoms. I'm told you fry in batter the male flowers, recognizable because they have no little potential squashes behind them on the stem.

What an idyllic evening that Friday night was. Janet had invited us to the Shakespeare Theatre in Stratford to see *Coriolanus*. The fun began with the three of us eating cold chicken, homemade orange bread, cheese and melon, and the Shrewsbury cakes, while sitting on a bank overlooking the water at Stratford and watching small boats come into dock. A gay and interesting crowd gathered for the play with a group from the UN in Eastern costumes, reminding us that we are not only national but international these days.

The play was stupendous. Because we sat in the second row we saw every breath and shared intimately every emotion, and they were numerous and violent. Coriolanus was a man who, like some of us today, couldn't bend—not one inch. Alas, the tree that can't bend in the wind cracks off in a storm, and so did he. This Roman aristocrat met his death because he couldn't yield, couldn't communicate or give where necessary and expedient to those with whom he was not in sympathy. Not only in Shakespeare's time but today we need to try our best to understand people with whom we are not in rapport, and to maintain friendly relations with those whom we disagree.

Those who say yes to life have a particular affirmative quality that shines from them. Janet is like this. She is always ready for anything. I remember one November on a cold and gray Election Day morning we called and asked, "Would you like to go voting with us?"

Janet, who had just wakened, said, "Of course I'd love to—and what do you think I should wear?"

"Wear? I don't think it matters," I answered wondering at her question.

"But I mean it will be cold on the water, won't it?"

She thought I had said boating! The fact that it was a cold November day didn't impede her enthusiasm at all. If we were going boating, she was coming too.

In view of this I wasn't surprised at her reaction to our phone call at nine p.m. on that beautiful evening, a few days after our Shakespearean adventure. Full moon in July came on a clear, warm night with no wind.

"Will you go swimming with us in the moonlight?"

'Certainly, I'd love it," Janet replied, "I'll be ready in a few minutes."

The air was balmy and soft and smelled of salt. Walking along the water's edge was a man playing "Greensleeves" on the harmonica and rather softly to himself. A huge red-orange moon rose out of the Sound sending a glorious shiny path over the water. We walked along the shore a few minutes appreciating the beauty, and the far-off quality possessed by that stretch of beach. We breathed the fresh, salt air, listened to the lap of the water, the swish of tiny waves along the sand, and the harmonica now playing the gay and rollicking melody of "Lillibulero." In contrast to summer afternoons when gay umbrellas dot the sand and children splash and call through the waves, the beach was now nearly empty.

We dropped our warm coats near the edge of the water and waded in. There wasn't a whiff of wind and the water was warmer than the air. The shimmering path to the moon reached out invitingly to draw us in ankle deep, knee deep and deeper. Where I swam the moon path stretched out in long, slim, horizontal strips, in smooth-folding streaks, in short staccato slivers, and in needle-prick sparkles. All these different textures blended together to form a silvery way that led out to where the black sky and black sea met.

"Do come over and see my path to the moon," I called to the others, "it is not like any I ever saw before, it is so bright and beautiful, and has so many different textures in it."

"I have one, too," Janet said, "and I'm sure yours couldn't be lovelier."

"I don't know what you two are talking about," laughed Bob. "The best path is mine over here." I looked across the few yards of water that separated the three of us, but I couldn't see either Bob's or Janet's path. Only my own, shiny and clear, leading out towards the horizon.

These July nights continue warm and lovely with the air so delicate it has the quality of a light touch on arms and face. These are wonderful nights for the beach, moon or no.

Another evening Bob and I drove down together for a swim and this time we went early to watch the sun set behind myriads of little boats at the yacht basin. The smooth shiny water picked up the gold from the sun and turned it to burnt orange as daylight faded. A few blue-black mackerel night clouds moved over the eastern heavens and the first stars pricked out.

We sat a while on the embankment and watched the life around the basin. A few ghostly white sails outside the harbor moved silently along as night sailors were enjoying the evening. A horn sounded as late comers called for the little launch to bring them ashore. A forest of tall catamaran masts rose slim and straight along the embankment on which they stood. A motorboat came in, found and picked up its mooring. A man with two teenage sons below us neatened up their boat, coiled the ropes and stowed the sails. Swinging a lantern they climbed down into the little dinghy and we could hear the splash of the oars and the boys' voices as they rowed ashore.

Over on the beach side there was no harmonica player tonight and only a very few cars. We watched one car spill out five small giggling girls who might have been eight or ten years old. It was somebody's birthday. The children slipped off their nightgowns to reveal brief little swimsuits beneath. They ran joyfully to the water's edge, giggled and splashed there where it was shallow while the two mothers watched from the car. Presently they all ran laughing back to the car, to their nighties, to their mothers, and drove off.

There was no moon tonight but starlight instead—and would there be phosphorescence? The water was still as glass with never a ripple. When we walked into it we suddenly became no longer earthbound but found ourselves wading through the Milky Way—yes, there was phosphorescence—and I never saw so much. As long as we moved and created a stir, be it ever so slight, countless stars were there in the water around us. When we stood still they vanished. While we swam myriads of glistening bits tossed off our arms, spread in rolling silver sparks, underwater and on the surface, endless and everywhere.

The separate definition between water, sky, stars, and our two figures swimming seemed to vanish. All merged into one. The whole universe was one, and I felt us lose separate identity and become one with it. In that instant I knew what the mystics mean when they say, "All is one." To be a part of such beauty for a brief moment was a rare and wonderful experience.

Such moments pass—but a little stardust lingers on your arms or in your hair.

Gaily we drove home, well wrapped, with the car heater turned on, and eating sweet, dark red, Bing cherries all the way.

8

August is the peak of summer

OUR NEWLY MOWN MEADOW lies flat and smooth and even while the fragrance of fresh-cut grass fills every room in the house. Windows are open day and night. We sleep out, often eat out, and in the evenings read on the screened porch. The freshness of outdoors is with us almost constantly.

The brook runs low, the dark water a mere trickle. Along the bank jewelweed stretches fleshy stems up through the shadows while charming delicate flowers spangle the foliage. When I was a little girl my friends and I used to make these blossoms into earrings, and play "grown up" in high-heeled shoes borrowed from my elder sisters' closets, sometimes with their permission, more often without. Now these many years later on a warm afternoon the neighbors' little girls, sitting on the grass under the shade of a spreading maple, string necklaces of jewelweed.

If July is a rose full out, August is a rose whose first petal has fallen. Everywhere is a sense of abundance but the abundance of a season completing itself. August is ripening grain in the fields blowing hot and sunny, the scent of tree-ripened peaches, of hot buttered sweet corn on the cob. Vivid dahlias fling huge tousled blossoms through gardens, and joe-pye-weed dusts the meadow purple.

Everywhere butterfly weed gives way to Queen Anne's lace, whose name comes to us from Henry VIII's day. During his gay revels, the King used to pursue the most attractive ladies of the court down the twisting paths of the famous maze at Hampton Court, causing shrieks of laughter that echoed back to the palace. When Anne became Queen, she heartily disapproved of all this, and ordered the maze cut down. Tulips, daffodils, and wild carrots were planted instead. And so, runs the tale, wild carrot acquired the name of Queen Anne's lace. The more sophisticated members of the court may have wondered at this roadside weed being brought into the formal palace gardens. But one of the charms of the new Queen was her love for simple things.

In August comes our one great Auratum lily, this season with eleven buds. The night before a bud unfolds the petal tips part slightly. Perhaps tomorrow I will get up early enough to see a flower open, I think. But even at seven I am too late. The new blossom is there pristine and perfect. Auratum lily petals are shiny and white as if made of wax, with a sprinkling of red-brown dots of color and a golden line at the center crease of each petal.

If we had twenty lilies and a garden to correspond, I would probably be too busy to contemplate one lily for half an hour. As it is, for the three weeks our one lily is coming and going, we don't miss a move. When Bob comes home from work we go out to see what is happening. We sit on the terrace sipping iced drinks before dinner and breathing in the scent. An Auratum lily full out is a miracle of beauty.

Summer flows on in its particular rhythm, seeping into our bones, painting colors over the landscape, bringing a holiday time, a time of relaxation, and of drifting through warm, languid days. There is a sense of continuity in these drowsy summer afternoons. You feel they will go on forever, and that you, too, will go on forever. But then a hesitation comes.

Out of the mist and humidity comes a day that is September—a day carved from ivory, cool and crisp and blue. Out of the midst of what is comes a hint of what will be. A single leaf turns red on the dogwood, and the goldenrod shows faint color.

August, like July, is a beach month.

One day our grandsons, Jesse and Jeff, were visiting and we three were sitting on the sand at Compo Beach. I was reading and both boys were stretched out nearby, talking together. Suddenly, what they were saying penetrated, and I came abruptly to attention.

"He's only in pollywogs," said Jeff.

"Two more tests and I'll be in shock," said Jesse.

"*What* did you say?" I asked in astonishment.

"Two more tests and I'll be in shock," Jesse repeated.

"What *are* you talking about, Jesse?"

"Yes, you see, Grandma," Jeff explained, "Jesse will be in shock and I have one more test and I'll be in flying fish."

"Where are you now, Jeff?" I asked, thoroughly confused.

"I'm in minnows."

And now Jesse took over. "It's this way, Grandma," he said patiently. "First you are in Pollywogs, then Frogs, then Minnows, then Fish, then Flying Fish, then Sharks, and by that time you are really a very good swimmer."

"Oh!" was all I could manage.

"Come on," said Jeff leaping up, "let's go and watch them fishing off the rocks."

"I'll race you," cried Jesse who was up and after him on the instant.

Like two streaks they were off up the curving stretch of beach toward the grass that rises up out of the water like a Japanese print. They ran on to where tumbled boulders reach out into the water, and to where three men were standing hip-deep and casting out their lines.

Did you ever watch the tide turn?

I had this very special experience at the end of another pleasant afternoon on the beach—a day when I had gone down by myself. It was gray and lovely. Sea and sky met with no sharp line dividing them. In the mysterious, misty area between the two, white sails appeared and disappeared. The water was velvety smooth and 70°. It felt like velvet, too. For a while I floated, letting myself drift, and now and then with a few easy strokes I moved a little one way or another. It was delightful looking out along the water towards the sails.

After a while I waded ashore admiring, on the way, the seaweed that floated just under the surface. Some bits were like miniature trees, green or red. When I picked one up it shrank into a damp string of red slime. But back in the water, in its proper element, it spread out again into a tiny fairy tree from another world, beautiful in each intricate detail. On the sand lay more seaweed, bright wisps of green twined around a variety with hard black bubbles that cracked when you pressed them. Dainty scallops lay next to wrinkled old oysters.

While I sat on the sand the whole scene seemed to have the quality of a painting by Seurat—the same gay umbrellas, women and children in bright bathing suits, reading, dozing, picnicking. The hum of voices, the calls of children, a laugh, a cry, a "watch me," a wail, a giggle, a snatch of serious talk, all blended into a kind of symphony. The dream quality abroad was heightened, perhaps, by the fact that, with no horizon line, the boats at times seemed to be sailing through the sky.

Now a castle emerged from out of the smooth flat sand near me under the shaping hands of a little girl in a blue bathing suit and a tangle of yellow hair.

I remembered a comment Jeff had made earlier in the summer. We'd both finished a picnic lunch and were sitting in silence.

"You wouldn't know, Grandma, would you, that there were all those castles in that smooth wet sand there? I mean the castles that aren't built yet."

This reminded me further of the small boy visiting the famous sculptor's studio who asked,

"How did you know that a lion was in that piece of marble?"

I looked beyond the castle down towards the water and realized the tide must be dead low. Nature seemed to be holding her breath before the turn.

Presently I experienced a little shiver of excitement. The beginning of a ripple moved over the water's surface, a pause, and then another. Each slight movement gathered force until finally a wave visibly emerged on the sand, leaving a faint rim of white foam. In a moment a second wave, then a third reached out, and the tide had definitely turned, was on the way in. Every wave now washed up a little further than the one before it, and, receding, left its wet scallop shape higher on the sand. What a great ocean of water slowly followed where but a single wave had first tentatively reached.

It was a day swept clean. I looked out at the blue sky and watched the wind tossing the maples along the stone walls. After hanging up an immense washing, answering a pile of letters, and getting dinner in hand, I rewarded myself with a book and the hammock for the afternoon. I lay there reading, dozing, looking up through the maples and watching the wind blow their tops. The trees around the terrace fairly danced. In my dreamy state I saw them first as herds of buffalo galloping over the western plains, next as waves on the great outer beach at Cape Cod, rolling and breaking. Then they were like girls bent over drying their long hair with wind and sun streaming through it.

The leaves tossed wildly, and even the large trees bent in the wind while their roots held firm. Because they bend readily, they spring back unharmed. What a delicate balance lies in yielding, yet holding firmly rooted.

Nature's weather moods creep into you, whatever their character, and something in you responds one way or another. There are forward-moving days when you step on ahead into new projects, clear crisp definite days whose shape you recognize when you first rise in the morning. You know what such a day will be and what you will do in it. Then there are quiet days when you move slowly in the rhythm of the hour with no special plan, no feeling of rush or push; you just go along happily but gently.

There are days of violence when a storm threatens, and when you respond by vigorously attacking things that need attention, closets, cupboards, difficult letters and tricky phone calls. Weather, when you live in the country, is so much more than the short notice in the paper, "fair and warmer" or "steadily rising temperature with a chance of showers." Every sort of weather finds some echo within each of us.

One night the full moon rises red-gold over the treetops and moves across the heavens turning silver as it goes. Riding high it causes dogs to bark restlessly, and we hear the hollow distant baying of the foxes in our hills.

The Swiss philosopher Amiel wrote a hundred years ago: "Tell me what you feel in your room when the full moon is shining in upon you and your lamp is dying out and I will tell you how old you are, and I shall know if you are happy."

I hear the sound of Bob sharpening the brush hook to scythe along the walls. The grating of the metal on the grindstone comes to me in the kitchen where I am cutting up squash to freeze. I always enjoy watching him scythe with his even strokes and a beautiful rhythmic swing. There is more to scything than meets the eye. I tried it one time and nearly cut off both ankles at once. Scything, I have decided, is my husband's department. A sickle I can manage with a quick twist of the wrist that Bob taught me, and it is quite fun. But scything, no. As Bob clears away the grass and weeds, the stone walls come again into view and nothing is more handsome than gray New England fieldstone walls. Theirs is a quiet dignity as they border our meadows and fields. They flow along the ground, up over a rise, down into a hollow, adapting to contours, leading the eye on and on.

One of the pleasures of midsummer is to stand in the vegetable garden or sit on the fragrant hay mulch and eat small red cherry tomatoes, while the sun shines on them and they are warm to touch. They are good in the house as hors d'oeuvres, but never to be compared with the way they taste when you sit beside them and pick and eat with the pungent scent of tomato foliage rising around you.

At this season countless volunteer nicotiana grow up and flower everywhere. Each night at dusk dozens of blossoms star the tumbled sea-green asparagus foliage, emerge here and there through rows of beets and carrots and peer around the cornstalks.

Even a dry summer such as this has its advantages. We are in the midst of what we might call "California weather." Day after day the sun shines, strong and bright. Everything grows furiously and the things you can water become veritable miracles of production.

We picked twenty-seven cucumbers from three hills in one week! In their abundance these cucumbers leapt up the fence to float runners across the tops of the asparagus next to them. Out of the middle of the asparagus come dozens of miniature tomato volunteers. Asparagus, cucumbers and tomatoes are good companion plants. Each imparts something to the soil desired by the other. For a great harvest plant all three near each other.

Our rhubarb, too, is reaching towards heaven. The chard is hip high. Out of the middle of parsley comes lettuce. Peppers are maturing, and potatoes. Four kinds of squash are burgeoning, yellow crook neck, green zucchini, butternut, and acorn. Three corn plantings are ripening in succession.

Our corn is as high as the Rodgers and Hammerstein 'Elephant's Eye,' maybe higher. Just now we are engaged in a battle with the coons who enjoy the corn as much as we. They laugh at our traps and walk around them. They are getting very clever as they come each night and eat the ripening ears. We are getting cleverer too, we hope. We shall see who wins the corn. So far they are ahead. Nearly all of the first planting has gone to them.

This is the most relaxing time of all the year in the garden. What vegetables and flowers we have planted are already there. Too late to think up other crops for this year. The glories of the present moment engage our attention and prevent any looking backwards or ahead. Even the bulb catalogues for fall lie unopened.

Every day is harvest day—every friend who comes leaves with cucumbers, squash, tomatoes. The garden is a jungle and we love it. It is full of mysterious surprises too. Out of a forest of cucumbers, beans and parsley, and for no good reason, comes the weaving stalk of a lone rose geranium with a single lavender bloom on the top!

August is also a vacation month and friends are constantly coming and going. The very curve of the road tantalizes and invites. Oceans beckon, hinting of exotic lands beyond the horizon. Mountains insist that you come and explore. We must reach out and discover what lies beyond our immediate vision. Something in us wants to broaden our base by exploring other areas and learning about far places. Many yield to this urge, and take off—far or near. Much as we love to go, how wonderfully happy we are to return home. If I have flown a long distance it takes me a few days after the trip to adjust to the time change and feel I am really home. They say that you will sometimes see a Hindu sitting at an airport for hours after a flight waiting for his soul to catch up with him. I feel for him.

We have evolved a particular and satisfying way of travelling. It would work anywhere but we happen to have perfected it in Europe. It is not actually the location that counts but the method itself.

I remember our first trip abroad a few years ago, when, like most inexperienced travelers, we tried to see too many things too fast. That trip taught us the theme of our present, improved way. Our current goal on a holiday is to see *more* of *less* rather than *more* and *more.*

We try to spend the first part of a vacation in a single place, usually a country inn in some area where the scenery and climate especially appeal. During the last part of it we explore new places at a slow and leisurely pace. There is an insidious nagging little voice from within that always urges "Who knows when you will be this way again, better see it all now, everything." This particular gremlin speaks to us too, but we don't listen any more. Not since we met a woman on the cog rail, ascending the Jungfrau. She asked in a dazed sort of way, "Pardon me, but what country is this? We're on a tour, you see, and we visited eleven different countries in the last seventeen days, and I'm sort of confused."

This memory keeps our itinerary simple. Last year we began our holiday in the small village of San Luc, Switzerland. For three weeks we settled down there, one mile high on the steep slopes of a mountain.

"You mean you never visited Rome and Florence when

you were so near, or even Salzburg, Vienna, or Berlin?" a city minded friend asked in astonishment after we got home. "But whatever did you do in the same mountain village for so long?"

What did we do?

Many days we did exactly nothing, but sit and read or perhaps just sit and absorb the surrounding beauty. Having no plan was what made it a vacation. We took long siestas in the afternoon, perhaps with a book under the pines. Often after breakfast we set out on foot with a picnic lunch. The invigorating mountain air seemed to lift us up to the high slopes. At the cow barns above the tree line they always gave us fresh warm milk to drink with our bread and cheese and fruit.

At the end of nearly three weeks of exploring this mountain region, of days passed in the bracing air, we were ready to drive about and see wonders created by the hand of man, the things we had read about during the winter—cathedrals, palaces, museums, paintings, sculpture, and even a city or two.

We limited the total distance of our last ten days of driving to less than 1200 miles. We drove in the morning, stopped for whatever caught our fancy, a photograph to take, a bird to identify, or a brief walk down an inviting lane. We always paused in some village to buy lunch—long European loaves of fresh, warm bread, cheese and fruit.

Our guidebook listed many magnificent cathedrals in the vicinity of Paris. We visited three. Had we seen half a dozen we would never have had the clear and rewarding memories we have of those three. It is a nine-mile walk through the Louvre if you see everything! We lingered there with a few works of art that were important to us, and spent the rest of the afternoon in a little sidewalk café near the Seine.

No, we have not seen Vienna, Berlin, Rome, or Florence—*yet.* Had we crowded any of these into our month last year, we would not have the lasting impressions and significant feelings about what we did see. The piggy-bank is ever at hand and the budget cooperates. These other places provide a fine incentive for saving and future trips.

If I were to sum up the rules for our carefree kind of travelling holiday, they would begin:

1. Gauge the whole trip to leave plenty of time each day for both a little sightseeing and resting, the latter being vital.

2. Reach your destination by early afternoon. This gives you a choice of hotels, opportunity to rest, and a chance to sightsee.

3. In the museums read and learn about what is there beforehand, if possible, and select only a few things that especially appeal to you. Linger with these and leave the rest for another day or another vacation.

4. Allow time on every trip, and interludes in every day with no plan at all, for yielding to the inspiration of the moment.

5. Resist with all your might the temptations that come all along the way to add extra miles and extra sights that are off your route, that will clutter your day, your week, and add unwanted mileage.

It has been said that you can travel outwardly into new places only as far as you are willing to travel inwardly into new places—and grow. When you never rush everything you see becomes more meaningful. Deeper levels within you, and some you never knew were there stir, waken, and stretch. You move closer to the heart of each area visited, and to each work of art seen—and perhaps you also move closer to your own heart.

How well I remember our return from that first trip to Europe. I was filled to the brim with the little Swiss mountain village where we had stayed so long.

"I can't wait to hear about your trip," said one of my good friends, and then rushed on to tell me about her summer. I never got a chance to say a word, or to share my feelings about any of the trip. Haven't you had this happen to you? Of course, I was so annoyed I wasn't more than half hearing my friend either!

Have we all forgotten how to listen these days? Not everybody, of course. Each one of us surely knows one or more warmhearted, interested, receptive friends to whom we can turn in time of need or when we have something to share.

A good listener is a warm and friendly person with a basic affection for people, a great capacity for understanding and compassion, and an ability and willingness to listen without waiting to snatch the conversation at the first interval. A good listener cares enough about his friend to want to learn what is important to him. He wants to become involved.

An exchange of this sort between two friends, or family members, deepens and enriches the relationship.

The bird songs of spring and early summer have given way to the rich sounds of many insects that live deep in the grass. They sing during warm August noons in rising crescendo, and fill summer evenings with their music. The katydids lead the chorus, loud and strong—lots of katys and a katydid, then more katys. Serious and solemn comes the barred owl—"Who-cooks-for-you, who-cooks-for-you-all?" The whippoorwill calls with steady persistence, and is echoed from afar.

The snowy tree cricket is another of our night musicians. Every evening, hidden high in the terrace maple, one of these little insects communicates with a friend in another tree. "Chee-chee-chee," he calls, and his friend responds in kind. Now a chorus of others across the meadow join in, and the night vibrates with their sounds.

Palmer's *Natural History* tells fascinating things about this half inch snowy tree cricket. In the first place, despite his name, he isn't snowy white but pale green with delicate long, back-swept antennae. The male secretes at the base of his wings a liquid that the female enjoys eating. If you add thirty-seven to the number of times the male calls in fifteen seconds, you get the approximate Fahrenheit temperature! Aside from these astonishing facts we can thank these little creatures not only for enhancing our warm summer nights but also for consuming quantities of aphids.

The imminence of Autumn is evident in the heavy white morning mist that bathes the whole world. It shimmers over the south meadow and, while you watch, disappears. Was it ever there? Yes, for its silver signature dusts the rose leaves, the asparagus, and the meadow grass. This is the month of seeds ripening. Gray milkweed pods grow fat. Fluffy cattails and downy thistles invite the birds. Along the roads and in the fields, and in all gardens everywhere, plants are maturing and tossing seeds to the wind for next year's growth and harvest.

In Nature's plan there is an abundance for wild life and for the continuation of the species as well.

This is the month when man listens and knows in his heart that there will always be planting and harvest. Always hills and meadows filled with things growing. Streams, mountains, and trees will always be with us. There will always be the life-giving sun, the beneficent rain, the changing seasons, and always endings that lead to beginnings—seeds and the springtime of planting them.

It is especially now that we are aware of the endless cycle of life and of its continuity. All of us have our uneasy moments realizing that science has advanced somewhat ahead of man's wisdom for the use of it. But when you look at Nature's harvest, her generous scattering of seeds at this time, you sense the plan and pattern back of all the visible world, and fears are replaced by a sense of confidence and basic faith.

Towards the end of the month Bob and I were out in the vegetable garden considering the corn that we might pick tomorrow or the next night, coons willing. Part of the after-dinner tour is to see what has grown in the vegetable garden. There were so many beets and carrots that they seemed to be pushing the earth aside to make room! We were standing on the deep and fragrant hay mulch in a state of beautiful content, such as comes to gardeners at harvest time, when we heard a honking overhead. Looking up we saw, wheeling across the sky, a great wedge of wild geese. Silently we watched these creatures of the wilderness. Following their instincts they fly unerringly in the right direction at the right season. Now we know that summer is ending. We will have warm days, we will have more swims. We will have all that goes with summer for a few weeks yet, but days are shorter, and signs are unmistakable.

A new season is blowing up the valley, drifting over the hills, rising up from a cooling earth, a new season with its challenges, its changes, its excitements, and its own particular rhythms and miracles.

PART 4

Season of gathering the harvest—of new energies, new directions

THE EARTH GROWS COOL to touch, the first sumac leaves turn red, and a new school year begins. One morning the air is crisp and cool and sharp. The scent of wild grapes drifts on the breeze with the pungent odor of chrysanthemums, and bright red apples ripening. Rich harvests of peaches, tomatoes, cucumbers, and golden pumpkins are everywhere evident. Great simmering kettles send their fragrances through home kitchens as shiny jars of jellies, relishes, and packages for the freezer stand row on row.

The air is like wine, squirrels gather hickory nuts, and the chipmunks we haven't seen for weeks are busy about something in and out of the weathered gray rocks on the wall where they live. Nature first hints delicately of winter ahead with a day that is chilly around the edges. Then we have Indian Summer weather. Next comes a cold night and a morning with white frost scalloping the green strawberry leaves.

Something is us responds to the flaming foliage and falling of leaves. We feel a surge of fresh energy as this new season is born. We too are ready for changes, and to move forward into new and untried areas of thought and action. A kind of preparation fills our days as we gather together our households and ourselves for new activities, new friends, new horizons.

9

September is rich and ripe and mellow

SEPTEMBER IS A SWEEP of dusky, purple asters, a sumac branch swinging a fringe of scarlet leaves, and the bittersweet scent of wild grapes when I walk down the lane to the mailbox. September is a golden month of mellow sunlight and still, clear days. The ground grows cool to touch, but the sun is still warm.

A hint of crisp freshness lies in the early hours of these mornings. Small creatures in the grass, as if realizing their days are numbered, cram the night air with sound. Everywhere goldenrod is full out.

In our kitchen this month the kettle simmers with grapes, peaches, blueberries, sending a wonderful aroma through the house while shelves gradually fill with neat rows of jams, jellies and juices. How pretty the jars look standing in rows on the kitchen counters cooling, especially when a beam of sunlight, shining in the window, lights the colorful contents.

When I was a child September was also a great preserving month, with even more laying aside of food for the winter. In our basement kitchen were great kettles, dozens of Mason jars in all sizes, stacks of rubber rings, and the smell of paraffin melting on the back of the coal stove. Over it all presided Delia, our Irish cook. Her apron, usually immaculate, was decorated today with a few streaks of golden juice. Her white hair was slightly askew, and a small smudge tinted her forehead.

Steam rose around Delia as she stirred the boiling kettles. My father's peaches, which always took all the blue ribbons for size and quality in the local fairs, stood in baskets around the room. Arthur kept bringing them in, sun-ripened from the trees. My father always insisted that none be picked until fully ripe. Preserves from tree-ripened fruit, he always explained, have a particular flavor that other fruit lacks. Actually he was quite right.

"I can tell the difference with my eyes closed," was one of his favorite comments.

And so can I.

On these preserving days I would sit hypnotized in a corner of the kitchen, watching. Delia tied one of her great blue and white striped aprons around me on the theory that I was helping. The apron was so large and starched that it really eliminated me from the scene of action by making it next to impossible to move.

While Delia stirred, and occasionally rearranged a great bone hairpin to keep her hair out of her eyes, she talked.

"Sure an' it was a great fair they had in Ballyshannon. I can see it as if it was today. Me mither polished me black-buttoned shoes, ironed me white apron and took me by the hand, and Sean McGillon next door drove us in his horse and cart. Sure an' if I didn't win the prize for the best God Bless Our Home sampler—a pair of little lambswool slippers, and I wore them to bed every night all that winter. Them were the days—." And Delia sighed, tightened her apron around her middle, and stirred a great bowl of sparkling white sugar into the kettle.

"Here, child," she said in a few minutes, "have a taste and tell me if 'tis sweet enough." Delia spooned out a few peaches into a small saucer, spread me a slice of homemade bread with homemade sweet butter.

She herself tasted constantly, which perhaps accounted for her rather large girth. To be asked for my advice made me feel taller than I was and quite content.

"Is it sweet enough, my child?"

"It's lovely, Delia," I would answer. But some days, wielding my new position as advisor, I'd put on a thoughtful air and say as imperiously as I could manage, "Maybe a little more sugar, please, Delia."

Into the great kettle would go one single spoonful, she would stir, and give me more to taste.

"Now it is just right," I'd say approvingly.

We both understood this little game, and it made the time with her infinitely precious.

I might be the baby of the family above stairs, but with her my prestige flowered.

On these preserving days our basement kitchen was the hub of my universe. From a high stool in the corner I could hear the sound of tennis balls being hit as my older sisters played outside on the grass court, and occasionally Bessie, our cow, in the far pasture mooed. My mother's voice drifted down as she and a neighbor sat on the porch above rocking and sipping homemade grape juice.

I was extremely comfortable with Delia, especially when we drifted back fifty years or so into Ireland. I developed quite a kinship for that little girl who wore shiny black buttoned shoes like mine, and a white apron. She became a very real friend of mine.

September, those many years ago, and today, may differ as to buttoned shoes, coal stoves, and grass tennis courts. But kitchens remain the center and heart of a home whatever the year or the generation. And September in any era has always been a time of preserving and conserving.

When you step out our back door you smell grapes. When you turn in the drive you smell grapes. In fact their scent greets you everywhere on our place. Today Mrs. Glover came and we made twenty-nine pints of grape juice. What a woman she is! What energy and stamina in spite of her eighty-three years. Is it because she works so much with her hands that she has a simple directness about her, and that her brain, uncluttered by too much learning, has remained clear and shrewd?

We sat on the terrace beside the rose bed and slid grapes off their stems into kettles. I next covered them with water, adding another inch over the top. After fifteen minutes of simmering, the skins and seeds separated from the pulp and Mrs. Glover put them through the colander. The juice dripped out and we tossed away the pulp, and reheated the liquid with honey. When sweet enough, and just about to boil, I took it off the stove and poured it in the roasting pan to cool. There is no magic about the roasting pan but I was running out of kettles.

All the while we made the juice we talked. Mrs. Glover is a wonderful person to exchange ideas with. She likes to speak of the olden times in these parts, and I love to listen. This seems to be the season of nostalgia for most of us, and of dreaming back to other days, other times.

I learned about the village of Valley Forge which used to be where the reservoir is. Mrs. Glover went to school there. She told me how all the girls rushed to get to school early. The first one to arrive was permitted to sweep out the room for the teacher while the earliest boy was stoking the stove.

Mrs. Glover taught me some of the garden wisdom that her father had imparted to her—wisdom we have since proved in our garden. Beet and carrot seeds sown in the waning moon are up and growing by the next full moon, and the young plants benefit from the rays shining on them at night. Pull weeds and cut down trees when the moon is waning. Start all new projects when the moon is waxing and set out new plants at this time. Mrs. Glover's final thought for that particular day was that moonlight bleaches sheets if they are left out a night or two.

When the roasting pan was filled with cooling juice I drove Mrs. Glover home and returned with a fresh dozen of her eggs.

Sarah, a good friend of ours who lives across the reservoir in Redding, came for dinner. We three ate baked swordfish, fresh garden corn, and afterwards sat on the terrace and consumed several bunches of grapes apiece. After a very gay time we all took to the kitchen and put the now cooled juice into containers and packed them in the freezer, admiring as we did so the mounting stacks of vegetables and fruits there. How we will enjoy these all winter.

In September the garden clubs convene again after the summer's pause. Everyone is home from vacations, telling tales of fabulous roses in England, large as grapefruit, rainbows in Geneva's Jet d'Eau, geraniums in Switzerland, almost too red to be real, and fields of scarlet poppies all through rural France. We also learn about sunflowers, bordering

America's western highways, camping beside snowbanks in Yosemite, and the charms of a holiday in a small Vermont village.

One of the excitements of the month is the Organic Garden Club Show. This year it was called the "Fête on the Green" and occurred at Greenfield Hill Church. The intent was to have it resemble a small country fair on a village street. Outside the church under the trees stood the booths forming two long rows. Over each booth was a gay striped umbrella, topped by even gayer balloons. The ground in the whole area was spread with fragrant hay. A great wheelbarrow spilling over with fruit and produce enhanced the entrance along with artistically arranged cornstalks, bittersweet, and pumpkins. The whole created an effective approach that was completely irresistible.

All week before the show members of various committees kept calling to see if I would help in this or that area. I ended up going into production on bread and meringue cookies. Both turned out rather well—the bread in spite of the oven conking out in the midst. The last two loaves, having risen as high as they could go, sat there sometime before I discovered the power was off. As soon as I realized I frantically moved them to the other oven. They sagged slightly but not too much. I had learned about the meringue cookies last winter at the Rug Hookers. They are the "One-One-One" cookies that take about five minutes to make, and all but float off the plate.

The day dawned and off I went with eight loaves of bread, several plates of cookies, and a great basket of plants for the plant sale. I also took miniature marigolds to exhibit, and three fabulous and fragrant bunches of Niagara grapes. Each bunch was huge, unbelievably beautiful. I had been watching these grapes for weeks with the show in mind, and hoping the coons would leave them, and happily, they did.

I also took tomatoes, and thereby hangs a tale. Bob and I were prowling around the night before, considering what I might enter and studying all our tomatoes. The large ones seemed pretty good but all had the common scars on the top that don't make a bit of difference in the eating but aren't good for a show. There was a special charm to some smaller ones, volunteers, that grew out of the midst of the chard. Each one was perfect, not a blemish. These were larger than the cherry tomatoes.

"They're about the size of ping-pong balls," Bob said, "they must be a cross between the ordinary large ones and the cherry ones. Say—why not enter them as Ping-pong Tomatoes?"

So I did, selecting three perfect ones, and they won first prize over all tomatoes, including many entries of the regular large-sized ones.

The grapes whose scent spread through the "village street" won a blue in the fruit class. The marigolds won a second. At the Garden Club Show, practically everyone wins a prize, and this is half the fun! It naturally puts us all in a wonderful mood. Inside the parish house we had music and tea and sold the food. I was happy to see the bread and cookies and all the delicious organic food selling fast. The day was a huge success. Even intermittent showers didn't bother too much or dampen spirits.

At one point we heard a great roaring truck along the road.

"Good Heavens," cried an agitated member in a real frenzy, "they are spraying the trees."

To have the Organic Garden Club's annual show of pure unsprayed vegetables and fruits in the shadow of a truck dispensing poisons would indeed be ironic! After a few bad moments we discovered the machine was vacuuming the trees, whatever that means, not spraying them. Quite harmless though mystifying!

A happy climax to the organic fete was a rain that followed. All night it poured. Next morning Bob, still in pajamas, rushed out to check the gauge. One and three-tenth inches—the most we've had in months. The world this morning is gold and silver with the sun pouring over the meadow. The earth is steaming and every plant looks fresh scrubbed and renewed. The rain brought out the purple asters in the meadow, blue gentians across the land, and everywhere goldenrod is a deeper yellow.

On a clear sunny day with a crisp breeze, out come the sweaters and wool skirts, and away go the summer dresses. I greet my beloved sheep-lined shoes which are so warm for driving, the hand-crocheted wool throw that my mother made, and some of my favorite winter dresses. The pleasant smell of cedar permeates the house, as Elsie, who comes every week to clean, sprays closets and helps hang Bob's suits out in the sun. The loveliest dresses of last summer now are less interesting than the rich dark greens and other winter tones of the clothes I haven't seen in months.

It is pleasant to greet again the woolen scarf I bought in Switzerland and my favorite Swiss mittens. I had forgotten about them. This needs a stitch and that needs a hem change. So I settled on the terrace to sew for the new season.

While I sewed I began remembering Mrs. Kramer out of my past. This month the house where I grew up was always filled, not only with the scent of preserving, but with the hum of the old-fashioned foot-pedalled sewing machine up in the guest room. Mrs. Kramer, our itinerant seamstress, used to come every September and settle in for several weeks to make fall clothes for the whole family. She always gave me countless little scraps of material which I treasured. Delia, on her Sunday off, would often make me doll clothes out of them—Mrs. Kramer was not that type. She was a lady of temperament whose most frequent comment to me was, "Run along, little girl, don't you see I'm busy?" I would peer in the door crack and watch her with a mouthful of pins, sort of chewing them around, as she wielded a great pair of scissors through yards and yards of tulle that swathed the room. She sighed often, constantly talked to herself. To me she was a woman of mystery who inspired awe and more than a little fear. After all, anyone who could eat pins!

It's rather pleasant the way the human mind slips backwards and forwards through the years. What an interesting personal storehouse from the past each one of us has to revel in and to draw from. Sometimes a scent, an activity, a name, an object carries us back.

I have just witnessed a small miracle, and even better, I've had something to do with it. It all began at the last garden club meeting where we learned about drying flowers for winter bouquets. I had long heard of this process but it had seemed chancy and arduous and extremely complicated. But Marion, the member who was telling us how to do it, made it all sound so easy that the next thing I knew I was home with a few items from the florist shop and a five-pound can of Silica Gel which looks like salt with a few blue crystals in it.

The general idea is to pick flowers when they are opening and almost full out—never when they are passing or the petals will fall. At this late date my choice was limited to marigolds, zinnias, deep blue clematis and asters. The first three came out beautifully but the delicate asters lost their petals in process.

The method I learned is simple and fun. Take a large kettle with a cover and some lengths of slightly stiff florist's wire. Use only the flower head. Cut this off, run a piece of wire through the blossom, bending it and drawing it back so that you have a live marigold on an artificial wire stem. Next scatter an inch of Silica Gel on the bottom of the kettle. Stand the flower on its head in this and cover completely with more Silica Gel. Follow the same process with all the flowers until the kettle is filled. None must touch another. After two or three days gently dust away the powder, and the flowers, a little smaller than original size, are stiff and dry and, miraculously, as brilliantly colored as when they grew in the garden!

I bought some vases at the Five-and-Ten and some plasticene to hold the stems in place, and made a number of little bouquets for the house and for gifts. Interesting pods and grasses from fields and woods added charm to the arrangements. How pleasant it will be in January when a blizzard descends to have our bright red garden zinnias and yellow marigolds indoors.

Today at breakfast time we had no strawberry bed, by noon we had one—composed of twenty-five thriving bright green plants. It began at Paul and Frances' house. For a long time we had been admiring our friends' home-grown strawberries and wanting a bed of our own, but when we had tried some years before the birds had eaten every berry. Now the fine wire cover Paul had made, light and easy to move, converted Bob. We were going to try again.

"Today is a good day to move the strawberries." Paul said on the phone. So over we went with wooden flats and trowels. The Mooneys' organic vegetable garden is fabulous. We came home not only with twenty-five strawberry plants but enough Kentucky Wonder beans for one dinner to eat, and four in the freezer.

"I like them old," Frances said, "because then you can enjoy the flavor of the little beans within the pods."

This was a new idea to me who picks everything young. But I cut them small and the beans within *were* heavenly. We also brought home a huge bag of apples picked from the ground under their tree. We had applesauce all week, and pie for the week-end. Another treasure was a cantaloupe that had been lying in the hot sunny hay mulch. You could smell it three feet away, and the meltingly delicious flavor was superb!

This is the way with September harvests—half the fun of growing things for all gardeners is the subsequent sharing.

Back home we pulled up some ripe beets and onions to make room for the new bed. After loosening the soil we set the strawberry plants. Bob put water in each hole on the roots before covering them. This is our system to prevent the wilting of new transplants.

Later in the day we drove up to the reservoir and brought back two bushel baskets of pine needles for mulch. Strawberries have a special affinity for pine needles.

One day I looked at the greenhouse and really saw it. During the summer it gently sleeps, the green ivy a pleasant sight through the glass doors that connect with the living room. The greenhouse is there but I don't think about it much or do anything except water the ivy every morning. But now one September morning I saw it. I saw it as it will be filled with plants and with the orchids all flowering. Then I remembered the house plants summering along the edge of the asparagus bed. All have grown mightily and some are practically hidden under the asparagus foliage. It is time to bring them all in. What a delightful occupation—repotting, pruning, generally grooming them and creating an indoor garden in the greenhouse.

The gardenias given me by a friend last spring because the buds dropped in her house, are covered with fresh buds. Gardenias are tricky—will they flower for us? Each aurora borealis plant has become a small bush. The little azalea, from another friend at Easter, is covered with new leaves. Will that too flower again?

On a bright sunny day I settle beside the compost to pot up everything and make new cuttings. The compost is rich and black and feels good to handle. A little compost, a little garden soil, and some sand, all strained through hog wire netting, make a fine mix for most everything. I use more sand for the succulents, more leaf mold for the African violets.

Every aurora borealis plant makes about ten by the time I finish cutting it up. The geranium cuttings I pot don't bloom during the winter but by spring are ready for a summer's flowering.

Our orchids have been simmering down by the brook, luxuriating in the night mists that form above the water. They are the main features of the greenhouse, and I always enjoy getting them back under our roof again.

The urge that plants have to grow is exciting to encounter. When the greenhouse was rebuilt last spring I discovered some grape ivy in a dark corner under a bench, neglected there for years! It had lived, but never grown. I set it in the garden out of its container. Now when I come to repot it I was amazed. The thriving plant was covered with quantities of bright green shiny leaves. This year it will have a place of honor on top of the bench instead of under it. I'm rather ashamed to have neglected it so long.

Friday night the rain came and Saturday morning the air was crisp and sunny with a beautiful breeze stirring. We were eating breakfast when the phone rang.

"Do you think you could fly your kite on the boat?" Marjorie asked.

"We could certainly try it," was my response.

We started out with Marjorie and Ted on their cabin cruiser, taking sandwiches, fruit, fishing tackle and the kite. The sky was blue, the very air seemed blue and sparkling, and the deep blue water ruffled into little whitecaps. We went over towards Cockenoe Island, anchoring occasionally to fish. The fishing was great because we felt so many firm definite bites, but no fish. My delight over nibbles without fish proves, I guess, that I'm no true fisherman. The sea worms were horrendous creatures. The clean little hook-surrounded minnow that we used trolling was neater and less sinister, and equally successful at catching nothing.

Cruising along slowly we explored the bays of various small islands, and slid by sandpits where gulls had congregated in flocks and nestled, heading into the wind. Now and then one would fly up and return, again to face the wind.

We ate sandwiches in the warm sunny cockpit. It was a pleasure to watch Ted at the wheel and see the look of deep content on his face as he guided the boat. Bob wore the same expression when he took over. As skipper, Ted appeared to feel every mood of the motor, with his ear tuned to each throb.

Here on the boat we are in a world apart—a world of

buoys, navigation charts, lighthouses, sandy stretches, gulls, other boats that leave a pleasant swell, and whose occupants wave in passing. Then there is always the sea and the wind. The salt wind on a sunny day seems to blow into you everything that you want, and blow out of you everything that you'd like to be free of.

At first the kite took off obligingly from the boat, but after rising up some fifty feet, a gust of wind sent it nose-diving into the blue water. It received a thorough baptism as Bob reeled it in, wet and dripping. Later, back on the beach he sent it up again. This time it never faltered, but rose steadily up and up, and he could hardly let line out fast enough. A few curious gulls dived towards it and then slid off to the side, figuring no doubt that this was too large an enemy to tackle.

The whole sky was a tossing mass of cumulus clouds, a wonderful backdrop for the colorful kite. Bob kept letting out more line until it was up a thousand feet or so. Marjorie and I took turns with Bob and Ted holding the line and feeling the pull, the wind vibration, and the pleasant sense of being related to the upper air.

This was the day for the last swim of the season. We'd had several 'last swims' all month but this was really it. The wind blew and we had goose pimples, but the water was warm once you were in. A breeze kept sending little puffs over the dark blue surface, and off towards the horizon many small sails were billowing. We took a long walk down the beach with the kite in the air above. Marjorie and I were enjoying the hard wet sand just above the water line when we noticed some marvelous patterns sketched by the receding tide. Great peaked mountains, one behind the other, stretched on and on. We stopped some friends to show them these fabulous shapes.

"Oh, yes," said one, "looks like a river basin in Missouri in flood season." They seemed bored with the whole idea and didn't see Tibet and the Himalayas that were so obvious to us. Magic probably inhabits different realms for each of us.

Bob and I were eating supper at home after our day on the water when we heard the radio speak of frost.

We'll just let things (except tomatoes) freeze, we told each other nonchalantly. After all you can't resist fall, can you? This year we have had two weeks of grace. The first killing frost often comes about mid-September. After supper Bob called Mr. Follett and Mrs. Follett said he was out bringing in his tomatoes because of the imminent frost.

We put on sweaters and went out with baskets and flashlights to pick all the tomatoes and eggplant and peppers and squashes. We set the tomatoes in the shop on newspapers and an impressive row they made. I next cut a large bouquet of roses.

"Maybe after all we should save just a few things—do you think?" I suggested to Bob tentatively as I brought the roses in.

But he was already heading for the old sheets and tarpaulins that we keep for the purpose. We covered the ping-pong tomatoes, the little cherry tomatoes, and the miniature marigolds on the terrace and at the front door.

Next morning the fields were white and the temperature 30°. The sheets and tarpaulins lay stiff and white over the new strawberries and the tomatoes. As the sun rose the sweet potato vines that had been alive and thriving yesterday turned a slippery dark olive green. The tomatoes trailed limp leaves. By afternoon both were black and collapsed. The cucumbers went, the squash. But all around the house the bright yellow marigolds, saved by covering, caught and tossed back the sunlight.

It is pleasant to have friends you don't know as well as those you do. Any writer always receives a number of letters from readers, and this month, after a summer lull, a variety have come in. My letters usually question where to buy this or that. Sometimes, of course, a person hotly declares that I have a Latin name wrong. Occasionally someone wants to share a legend about a plant or tells me about his or her garden. The nicest letters say how much something I have written has meant.

I like to sit here among our flowers and vegetables and consider the other gardeners over the country also growing things, and experiencing the same rewards and pleasures, When my articles or books link us and a sharing occurs I am delighted.

As my birthday comes along this month a number of people phone or write, adding to the general air of festivity. On that day Bob came home early with interesting packages, and Sarah joined us for dinner. We ate steak and huge pieces of sponge cake I had made in the afternoon. Packages and presents are always exciting and we had a wonderful evening, including a walk up the road under the stars. No glowworms tonight—the frost has sent them underground—but stars were never brighter.

A child covets each birthday, but not so with every adult! My father, who seemed impervious to age, used to say that you made your own age whatever it was in years by your point of view about it. There are also those who, during the second half of life or even before, put on long faces and begin closing doors. They sigh and say, "It's terrible to grow old—can't do the things I used to."

These people constantly talk about what they can't do and dwell on their limitations. Then there are those who, like the insects this month, seem to feel their days are numbered, and cram every minute. They rush and rush and never light anywhere long enough to really feel the activity at that spot.

Fortunately there are others, and we all know them, both men and women, who dignify the second half of life by their attitudes. They move along a middle way at a leisurely pace, taking what comes in their stride, doing less perhaps, but engaging in each venture on a deeper level, more thoughtfully, and with greater awareness.

My friend Lillian who died a few years ago was one of these. In her late seventies she had attained a degree of serenity and wisdom that drew all people to her. She seemed never to close any doors but was always open to new people, new activities, new places, and best of all to new ideas. She never stopped learning and studying. Nor did she ever feel that she had to convert others to her particular ways of thinking.

"You know," she said to me once, "growing older is quite a relief. I used to think I would be a great artist, and I really worked at becoming one. But I know I'll never be famous and I couldn't care less. These days I paint for pure pleasure, and it is much more satisfying."

She also went on to say how rewarding it was to have lived long enough to see how certain things came out. She had seen various situations at their beginnings, watched the people in them grow, and observed what happened.

"Perhaps," she said, "the wonder of it, and what showed up throughout was the infinite ability of the human spirit to cope."

My father right up until he died in his eighties never lost his sense of wonder about people, events, nor his reverence for all of nature.

His last fall he was planning a new perennial bed, setting out more fruit trees. He was digging in new bulbs, and marvelling at autumn colors on an afternoon only a few weeks before he left this life.

I've often thought that it might be pleasant to grow old in China. I understand that the older you grow there the more you are consulted and the more wisdom is attributed to you whether you have it or not. This would be delightful! But I guess it is too late to be a grandmother in China now!

Although we are supposed to grow wiser as we grow older the younger generation seldom turns to the older for wisdom. Young people want to make their own mistakes in their own way, and we parents have to let them with as good grace as we can. I used to think if they would only listen and follow *a little* of our "adult wisdom" their mistakes would be on a higher level. But I see this is impossible.

It has been comforting to realize, though, that after our children developed their own points of view, and became engaged in their own adult lives we could then begin to exchange ideas with them and amiably agree or disagree on a variety of subjects which we never could have even discussed when they were in their late teens. Even more delightfully miraculous, these days they occasionally ask our advice, although of course they don't always follow it. It is probably better that they don't. If life teaches anything it is that each person has to follow his own path. Nor can anyone ever see the way of another any more than he can see another's path over the water to the moon!

Last evening we were out scavenging grapes. After frost they are sweet as honey. Bob climbed the stepladder with the flashlight and handed them down to me, three here, five there. The stars were bright as we stood beside the arbor eating them. I think there never was such a night, nor were the stars more brilliant. The Big Dipper lay stretched over Pop's Mountain, and the North Star twinkled cordially.

The air is clear here, and with no city lights, stars are bright and numerous. All of a sudden one star began moving away from those around it. At first we thought it was a plane. There had been a plane a few minutes before, but the motion was different, and there was no red light. It moved as Echo did, with a slight hesitation, but kept going. This one was as large as the stars in the Dipper and equally brilliant. While we watched, and after it had gone some distance across the sky towards the northeast, it began to fade and suddenly disappeared.

"It must be a satellite," said Bob.

Next morning he called the Planetarium and they gave him a list of satellites to be seen all week, locations and hours, but said that there definitely had been *no satellite visible* on the night before at any hour.

My next thought was a flying saucer! These I am particularly fond of although I've never actually seen one. Flying saucer or not, how much more is up there than we understand or know about! Dealing with the practical aspects of living during the day, as we do, it always is a quickening experience to be caught up by the mystery of the universe under the stars at night.

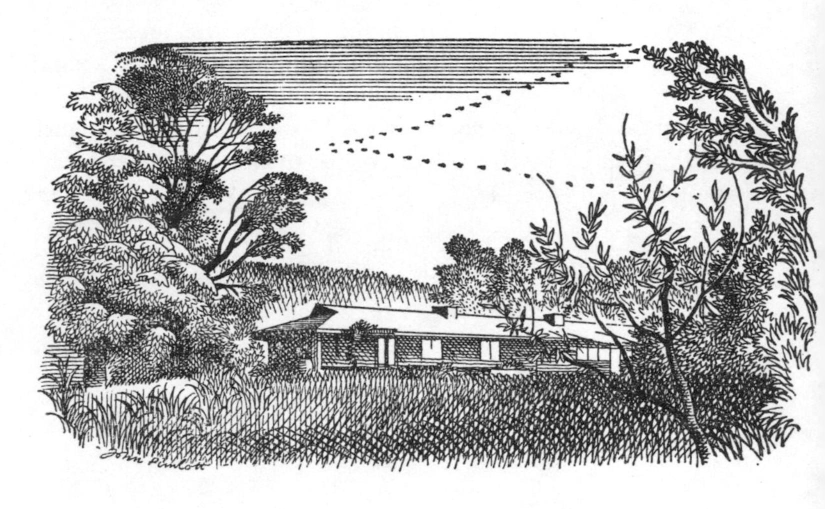

10

October is blue smoke and blowing leaves

OCTOBER ARRIVES in a swirl of fragrant blue leaf smoke, the sweetness of slightly frosted MacIntosh apples, and little hard acorns falling. We are in the midst of cool crisp days, purple mists, and Nature recklessly tossing her whole palette of dazzling tones through fields and woodlands. Our yellow maples around the house cause the rooms to glow till the very indoors air itself seems washed in gold. After a rain the damp tarred roads also shine gold. Where there are puddles you see sharp, clear reflections of bright overhead foliage. October is a time of glory wherever you look, up, down, or around.

About mid-month comes the climax, two or three days that you know are the peak—days in which the whole landscape is drenched in breath-taking hues. The crimson swamp maple at our entrance is so giddy in the sunlight that my heart skips a beat as I look at it. Everyone who lives in these parts or visits here catches the delirious mood.

We forget from year to year how stirring fall colors can be. Annually we tell each other these are the very best we have ever had. And this year they really are! No one has any adjectives left. The scientific-minded speak of pigment and chlorophyll, the rest of us just surrender to our emotions.

The fragrance of burning leaves is another autumn delight. Their delicious rustle and the scent of their smoke invariably carry me back to the days when my father used to rake great piles to burn. Before he lit them my friends and I would burrow deep and hide ourselves in the slightly scratchy heaps. From here we would look out at the world through tiny odd-shaped chinks of light. My father would build several immense piles taller than he, and call us out when he was ready for the bonfires. We'd stand beside him while three fires burned at once. He always did things in a grand manner—never just one fire at a time. Enthralled and slightly awed we watched the blowing feathers of blue smoke circle heavenward, and now and then a great volcanic eruption would mushroom out, followed by a roar of flames as a new part of one of the heaps caught fire.

We don't rake leaves where we live. Quite inadvertently, we put our compost in an angle of the two connecting stone walls in the northeast corner of our land. The prevailing southwest wind sweeps the leaves across the meadow—and right up to the compost—and we never need to rake a one!

I especially like the part of our place where our three compost piles stand. One is always in the making, one partly decomposed, and a third ready to use. About every six months each one gets turned over onto the next. After some months the leaves and weeds regenerate and become rich dark crumbly humus. This pure "gold" provides strength and new growth wherever spread. The compost feels good to touch and handle as I repot an occasional house plant. It smells good too, but is cold these days and my fingertips feel frosted when I finish.

Although leaves everywhere are falling, myriads of subtle signs of life abound. Tight little dogwood buds of next spring's flowers are revealed. Along each maple twig lie hard but promising nubs that will expand into next year's leaves. There is magic in the milkweed fluffs that blow their beauty out of twisted gray pods and transform the roadside. Each downy puff, drifting on the breeze, carries its miniature brown wafer of life to a new place to sprout in the spring.

We think of autumn foliage as being red and yellow but today we saw some that was blue. Some of the maple-leaf viburnum has pigment on the surface of its dusty pink leaves that is definitely blue, and from a distance creates a magnificent lavender effect. Over the week-end we walked up through Indian meadow to the reservoir and home over Pop's Mountain where ghostly white ferns haunted the shadows under hemlock and laurel. Oak leaves were golden copper in the sunlight, and half-round wafers of fungi in tiers one above the other, and in marvelous patterns decorated fallen logs and stumps. What grace and beauty nature displays even when disposing of dead and dying material.

Three great mushrooms stood together under a small laurel bush. Their underpleatings were snowy white and we admired their graceful curves. We are never quite sure when a mushroom is poisonous so we kept our distance. We brought home fern fronds to try to identify, and the leaves of some trees we didn't know. One long interestingly toothed leaf turned out to be a chestnut.

As we swung along under the colored canopy of oak and maple and beech interspersed with rich dark hemlocks, the air was fresh and cool. We stepped from rock to rock over rushing streams. Through the trees we presently glimpsed the reservoir bordered by great gray cliffs. We paused in a birch grove to look off over the blue water and to listen. In the silent forest behind us leaves fell and sounded like rain. One small curious chickadee chirped in a nearby tree. With a whir a frightened partridge flew off, and a sheaf of dry leaves blown by a chilly breeze rustled over the rocks.

I've just been out in the greenhouse watering the orchids and breathing in their sweet and sometimes spicy scent. People generally don't know that orchids are among the most fragrant of flowers. As cut flowers they usually have been refrigerated for days and are odorless, but on the plant and growing they scent the whole area. This is one reason why they are a joy to grow.

At least ten or maybe more times a day I find myself in the greenhouse and I am never quite aware of having gone there. Dreadful things can happen while I am happily discovering a new green-tipped rootlet reaching out through the side of a hanging orchid basket. Maybe a new bud is forming, one not there yesterday. On another plant a fresh flower is opening and, as I watch, the petals part.

Horrors—here is a sowbug! I get the bug bait that smells delectable—rather like licorice—and lures these creatures to their doom. By now the breakfast eggs have boiled to picnic hardness, the toast may well have burned, or a mid-morning hour has slipped by in which I was supposed to be somewhere else. I have become a rather unreliable character since the new orchids are installed in the new greenhouse.

My friend Mary and I have wonderful free and wandering days together through this Indian Summer weather. Every week for one day we turn our backs on all "musts," and "ought-tos" and declare a complete holiday. Since we both love and grow orchids we are usually drawn orchidward. Last week we took off with a picnic lunch for Lager and Hurrell in New Jersey. After exploring the state rather thoroughly, and browsing along all the parkways in sight we finally came upon the long sought Morris Avenue. But the numbers were in the thousands and growing higher every few blocks and we only wanted 426.

"Never mind," said optimistic Mary who is as hazy about directions as I, "the numbers will eventually have to get smaller."

But the numbers never did get smaller, and Morris Avenue turned to be Morris Avenue in the wrong town!

I often wonder what inhabits my mind in the area where most people's sense of direction resides.

"You can't possibly miss it," everyone said when we'd asked directions.

They'd have been surprised at the number of traffic lights we could miss, at the hospitals, schools, water towers, rivers, bridges, and other significant landmarks we never found.

In spite of all this, eventually we reached Mr. Lager's greenhouses and stepped into his tropical jungle, and there we completely lost our heads. Walking along the rows between benches loaded with plants we wanted them all. I succumbed to the charms of the tiny lavender Candlestick orchid, and to Gongora galeata with flowers like a small golden waterfall. Several great Cattleyas with swirling patterns in the throat of each flower proved irresistible. Other plants I brought had names a mile long like Odontoglossum pulchellum, Oncidium ornithrythum.

We started home, each with a large box of new orchids. After I left Mary and her plants in Bronxville I looked about at mine and felt that I had a carload of new friends. As usual I had more than I had intended to get. Then in addition Mary had given me ten beautiful plants that she said she didn't have room for.

"Where *are* you going to put them all?" Bob asked when he came home.

Some weeks before we had agreed that in the new greenhouse we would stress quality and not quantity. We would grow fewer plants, would study individual needs and grow each one to perfection. After all the greenhouse is only 12 x 10.

Our principle is, by special methods of simplification, to keep gardening "carefree" both outdoors and in. But in this instance I hadn't counted on the power of an orchid, and my inability to resist! Before long Bob was deep in it too, as we both unwrapped and arranged the new plants.

I sat up half the night looking up the unfamiliar varieties in seven orchid books. Quite a few were new to me. Did they like sun, shade, lots of water, high humidity? In which part of the greenhouse would each do best? The temperature varies 5 degrees from front to back. I fell asleep with my mind a beautiful confusion of Brassavolas, Steppoglottis, Vandas and Laelias. Laelia is a name I particularly like, it has such a pleasant sound as you repeat it. It may not be as useful to have all these names and orchid facts drifting around in my mind instead of a sense of direction but it is a lot more fun.

The orchid books have become my regular bedtime reading. By morning I seldom remember all I have learned but perhaps the process of repetition and studying will help me to master some of these names and needs and I hope I'll be able to attach the right need to the right name!

The remaining question is how will I keep on with my life when an hour has a way of dropping right out of the day, or sometimes two?

At present we are living out the Bible promise that to him that hath, more will be given. The greenhouse is filled with plants. I keep thinking we haven't room for a single additional one. But every few days some friend says: "I have an orchid given us last winter and it isn't doing very well. I don't want it to die—will you take it?"

So, strange and exotic extra orchids keep coming our way.

"But where *will* it all end?" Bob asked as I screwed in cup hooks and hung the last two gift orchids down from the roof. I wonder myself.

The effect is rather great, however, of orchids on the benches around three sides, and orchids hanging in the air above. When I mist-spray and the sun shines in, the fragrances rise—the scent of flowers mingles with the scent of growth. Time no longer exists there in this small personal rain forest—this built-in pocket-size jungle!

Down by our mailbox is the most fabulously beautiful and ancient maple tree. It must have been shaking down yellow leaves on the newly-landed Pilgrims. Surely it witnessed the British marching past here en route to Danbury. Today it is pure gold. Fallen leaves beneath it color the earth.

I was sitting on the bank across the road painting the scene. Wherever I looked what wasn't gold was scarlet and every shade in between. Trees were swinging a kind of glory in every leaf. The phrase "the power and the glory" kept running through my head. The glory lay visibly all around certainly, and the power? Wasn't that back of it all?

Could I catch in any small degree the mood of this dazzling spot on a piece of paper 10 x 14? Perhaps not, but I could try. After all, painting isn't wholly what happens on the pad but what happens to you while you paint. I can't draw very well, and my knowledge of perspective is hazy, but I love color. Mixing various tones and trying to reproduce even a small part of some appealing outdoor spot is rewarding in itself and great fun.

I hadn't painted in a year and that made it especially fine to sit on the bank and revive all the little ways of water color and brushes and sponges that I had previously discovered.

A number of years ago when the children were small I used to go out for the afternoon with an artist friend of mine. She would paint the landscape and I'd sit nearby on a cushion and read.

One day she said, "This is ridiculous, you could be painting too. Here, I've paper and paints for us both." Totally ignorant of the vagaries of water color I sat on the hillside filled with questions.

"What do I do first?" I asked.

"Use a lot of water and good strong colors. Choose a large brush and don't be picky and little about anything," my friend replied. "And I'm not going to tell you any more," she added briskly, "you will learn by experimenting."

"You mean you are not going to explain how I should begin?"

"Certainly not, you have to *feel it* yourself. You wouldn't feel it as I would so how can I tell you?"

I looked down at the little fishing shacks before us and the bay. We were on Cape Cod at the time. All I felt was panic. But, taking courage, I plunged in and began with blue sky which presently rolled off the paper onto my lap. Right away I learned two things—not to be quite that juicy and to hold the pad more level.

Over the next weeks my friend did break down and give me a few valuable hints but never very many, and that summer I developed a new hobby that has been pure delight during the many years since.

It is thoroughly absorbing and exciting to try to capture on paper a suggestion of sunlight patterns on the side of an ancient barn or tree branches blowing in the wind. There is usually at least one small part of each picture that conveys, to me at least, how I felt about the spot. This spurs me on to do another and another. Best of all I seldom forget the scene painted. It lives with me ready to be conjured up at will during any dull moment.

Bob has made a sort of "gallery" along the 14 foot wall of the study. Here a rack holds five pictures. Each has a mat and glass in front of it and slips into grooves top and bottom. It takes but a jiffy to change a picture. We can have a show of Mexico, Guatemala, California, Arizona, Switzerland, North Carolina or New England—all the places we have visited and where I have painted. We change exhibits frequently, and it is rather great to come home and in a few seconds have a new scene up on the wall.

We hobby painters are in good company what with the

late Sir Winston Churchill, ex-President Eisenhower, and a number of others. Among the interesting side effects of landscape painting is the fact that wherever you settle with pad and brushes people stop to talk. Painting is a wonderful way of making friends. Even in our remote area that morning a man stopped. He was an elderly photographer, and was taking pictures of the two horses that belong to our new neighbors across the street. While I worked we discussed foliage and fall and the photo essays he and his wife did of the four seasons. I was taking orange, scarlet and gold straight from my box of tempera and not mixing anything with them, but still on the paper they were pale beside the dazzling leaves that kept drifting down into the paint box and onto the pad.

Walking home later I happened to look up through the trees and then and there I stopped. Did you ever lie on your back in autumn and look up through tall trees at the sky? The red and gold leaves are magnificent against the blue, and the tree trunks all appear to converge towards the center, making a fascinating pattern rather like the spokes of an old wagon wheel. The best view was from the middle of the road —so there I settled. I'd lie on my back and look up, then sit up and paint what I saw, then repeat. This was fine until an oil truck came along, fortunately in one of my upright moments so I saw him first. He amiably and skilfully skirted my jar of water, the paints and me. Everyone always is friendly towards those of us who paint.

That night I put up five new paintings. Then I installed the equipment in the car. Any time, anywhere that I see something irresistible these autumn days I'm going to stop. I'll have to set out early for wherever I'm going, and I wonder if I'll always get there!

I was standing beside our parsley that was thick, abundant and bright green in spite of several hard frosts. I can be reckless about money at times but then suddenly my Scotch ancestry rises up, and it did there in the garden. I would have to think up some way to use all this valuable green so it didn't go to waste. I had already cut up and filled several plastic bags in the freezer for winter seasoning but all this was left over. Thus parsley Vichyssoise was invented.

Take a great handful of parsley, one boiled potato and some of the potato water. Add a little soup, made from chicken or steak bones, a small chopped onion. Put all in the blender and watch it gradually take on the delightful color of grass in the spring with the sun on it. Chill it in the refrigerator all day and you have a lovely Indian Summer guest luncheon menu or a dinner first course, hot or cold. Before serving, stir in sweet milk until it thins to your desire. Add a dab of sour cream, chopped chives, and a scattering of paprika. A bowlful is delicious and beautiful. Parsley is not only full of iron but especially high in vitamins A and C, so, as well as eating something delectable, you are also doing yourself a favor.

Last night we served a refreshing drink before a company dinner, something new and different introduced to us by a California friend. Pour a glass of Hawaiian Punch into a blender, a few mint leaves, a wedge of lemon, skins, seeds and all. Blend until no sign of lemon remains. Remove from the blender and add three more glasses of Punch—more if it's too tangy, less if it is too sweet. If you haven't a blender or are in haste, squeeze a half a lime into each glass of plain Hawaiian Punch. Either way it is ambrosia.

Every time I go to get a lamb chop or a garden vegetable out of the freezer I have to shift the autumn leaves around. They are beautiful, though, and quite worth it. I gathered several handfuls a few weeks ago and put them neatly one on top of the other in plastic bags. In the freezer they keep forever. We will probably not put them to this 'forever' test but use them to decorate the Thanksgiving table next month.

The freezer simply burgeons with small round plastic bags of our vegetables, frozen all during the summer. The last garden vegetables that we are picking outdoors now are particularly choice, perhaps partly because they are the last. They include Swiss chard, carrots, beets, our delightful celeriac and parsley. We had one meal of salsify. It was interesting but not exactly wonderful. The dry weather affected the growth and each root was too slim. The flavor, however, was different from all other vegetables and because it was our new experiment this year we enjoyed it.

The chard thrives beyond many freezes. The carrots are superb. Their orange tone is deep as autumn leaves and the flavor is rich and sustaining. The carrots you buy are insipid beside them. We shall leave these in the ground for the time being and dig them as we need them. The celeriac is delicious cut up in salad. This is the first year we have grown it, and it is a must for next season. After several frosts the parsnips grow sweeter and sweeter. It's only now that we've begun to buy some of the vegetables we don't grow such as artichokes, cauliflower, celery. All summer we used the mid-rib of the chard leaves as celery. This is great in chicken salad; in fact, wherever you use celery. It is especially good with olives as hors d'oeuvres.

Our flowers are all gone now except for a few pansies and johnny-jump-ups, and both seem frost-proof. On the terrace we also have some verbena in all the brightest colors along the warm south house wall. The indomitable dandelions keep opening their furry gold flowers through the lawn.

Shopping in Westport today was unusually pleasant. In every store people seemed to have time to talk. Perhaps that was because I was in no hurry myself, and also Wednesday is not a busy morning in town. Tom Messex from the hardware store stopped me on the street to say he had peas up six inches.

In spring our favorite topic of conversation is the state of our separate pea crops.

"But why this time of year, Mr. Messex?" I asked.

"Some got overripe on the vines and reseeded themselves," he laughed.

"You'd better cover them with plastic," I said, "and eat them for Christmas—that would be novel."

In Westport Food Center I got three dozen oranges and they were heavy. I asked if someone could carry them out to the car, and the new young man in the vegetable department came forward.

"The car isn't far," I said, "just across the street."

"That doesn't matter," said he cheerfully. As we crossed over he added, "I'd carry anything anywhere today—miles or mountains wouldn't matter—I'm feeling that good."

As he arranged the oranges in the back seat he said, "We've had a present at our house," and he whipped out of his pocket a leather picture wallet, and flipped it open to show a picture of a brand new baby. The young man stood inches taller and beaming all over with joy and pride.

"Your first?" I asked after admiring the appealing little face with eyes tight shut from youngness and from being so unused to this world.

"Yes, my first."

"Well, he *is* adorable," I said, "what is his name?"

"Why Junior of course—"

How good these things make you feel—!

I had come to town without my glasses and so apparently had everyone else in the florist's shop. We all had difficulty reading the fine print to see which of the poison spray cans had Pyrethrum and Rotenone instead of DDT. Everyone joined in the discussion of which spray would solve the mealy bugs on our jade tree.

"Did you try soap and water?"

"Did you try taking them off with a toothpick by hand?"

"Did you paint them with alcohol?"

"Have you sprinkled tobacco on the top of the pot soil?"

The answer to all the questions was yes, but still we have

the little pests. I left with one of the sprays, trusting that it would be effective. The little potted tree given me by a friend some years ago is nearly three feet high. No matter what we do, it seems to generate mealy bugs, but oddly enough it also appears healthy, with leaves large and shiny.

After filling the car with brown paper bags of the week's shopping I went into Peck and Peck. A half hour later as I walked down the street with my package swinging from my hand I was humming and walking on air. Well-wrapped in tissue within the box was a lovely new blue and green challis dress to wear out to dinner. Is the female of the species trivial and light-minded to be so easily lifted in spirits by a new dress! Maybe so, but why not? Though I'm not near to becoming an angel they say that angels fly because they take themselves lightly!

We had seven people coming for dinner. I reached up high onto the shelf in the cupboard for the company goblets. These had belonged to my mother and they're rather lovely. They have gold rims and a gold band around the base, and a pattern of stars in the clear glass sides. While setting the table I began thinking about the fact that my mother had bought these glasses shortly before she died.

They seemed so unlike her practical nature. What I recall most clearly about my mother is how she pitched in and helped when any one of us was sick, how she mended clothes and shifted hems, knitted the grandchildren sweaters. Once she made salad for 100 people when Bob's sister was married at our house. These things she did with vim and vigor, to say nothing of supporting herself when she was alone by building and selling a succession of houses. All these aspects I knew and admired but I didn't know the woman who would have selected these romantic glasses. This side of my mother, alas, I never touched.

Does a little girl ever know her mother beyond the practical side that takes care and is concerned? My mother obviously had her fey side, as I think back to many little things that she did and said and to which at the time I paid little heed. I often feel that this woman, born shortly after Lincoln was shot and who had watched Emerson dig in his garden in Concord, had so much more that was wonderful to give than I ever sought or was ready to receive.

I wonder if many parents don't have a somewhat incomplete relationship with their grown children. They may have a great time when together, but don't share ideas half as often as, "Do you want a hooked rug for the hallway?" "What color would look nice on the bolster pillows?" "Can I help you make the curtains?" This is very pleasant and does build a mutual sharing on one level, but it is only one part of a companionship.

How can we surmount the barriers of parental concern and emotional involvement to meet with adult children in the realm of meaningful ideas? Perhaps one clue is to recognize that we don't have to agree with a person to love him, and we all get along better if we don't try to tell one another what to think.

This morning I made Adele Davis pancakes. Exactly what they have in them depends on how chilly it is in the garage. The freezer lives there, and I go out in my nightie and bathrobe and slippers to get some of our various organic flours out of the freezer. We have barley, soy, rye, whole wheat, cornmeal. We still have one of the old-fashioned freezers that are deep pits. The man who first designed these certainly didn't have a touching concern for the housewife's peace of mind. To find what I want I toss things from one compartment into the next, for the object sought may well be at the very bottom, and all the while my fingers gradually freeze.

The frost also seeps up through the bottom of my slippers. So when my toes and fingers are as cold as I can stand I bring in whatever flours I have in hand. Two or three different varieties greatly enhance the mixture. This marvelous recipe includes yeast and rises for an hour before you use it. When you pour the batter on the sizzling griddle it is alive with bubbly growing yeast, and quite bouncing. The pancakes are pure heaven with butter and Vermont maple syrup. The recipe for an ample breakfast for four is:

2 packages of powdered yeast
into 1 1/2 cups warm milk
Add
1 tablespoon molasses
2 tablespoons melted butter
2 whole eggs
sift into liquid
1 cup flour (here I get creative and make it a cup of mixed organic flours and never the same way twice)
1/3 cup powdered milk
1 teaspoon salt
1/2 cup wheat germ
Beat fifty strokes. Let rise covered and in a warm place for 1 hour. Stir and drop on griddle that is 380° to 400°. If you have no thermostat just be sure it sizzles as the batter goes on.
The batter will keep several hours in the icebox.

This is the month of great activity. Watching the leaves turn and finally fall is an exhilarating experience. Perhaps some of the force and energy of the brilliant colors enters into us now and we have the urge to stretch out and encompass the new and the different. Numerous courses start in adult education programs. Concerts begin, the ballet comes to New York. Lectures, study groups and garden clubs all burgeon with projects.

I usually get into too many different kinds of activities at this time of year. One day I realize I am skimming the surface of everything. There is but hollow pleasure in too crowded weeks. Real rewards come from engaging in fewer activities and experiencing each one more deeply. Loss of alertness and freshness of approach tell me to slow up. Life is best when it is a balance between activities and intervals of aloneness. In the intervals we are able to deepen the meaning of the activities.

The days I like the least are those when I pass through my environment superficially almost as if it were a stage backdrop. I scarcely see anything except what needs doing at the moment. Meals become just something to get and nothing has depth. This is living "two-dimensionally."

In contrast, when I am not pressed by a push of events I move more slowly and savor each moment. Every activity becomes a feature in itself and the simplest routine has its own joy. I feel the texture of the blanket when making a bed, and it is good. I feel the soil when I am repotting a houseplant and it is good. I listen beyond words to what people mean. I look at the sales person in the store and really see her. I have time to write the author whose book I have liked, and I telephone my dinner hostess to tell her how much we enjoyed the evening. This is living "three-dimensionally"—going that extra mile, doing all the things you are not required to do, but which give added meaning.

Living this way you see not only your goal but the path that leads you there and all the little flowers and ferns that grow along its edges.

Our meadow was frosted white this morning and the early temperature 28°. The sun was brilliant and by ten it had warmed up. Bob is painting the house. While he brushed on the color I worked on the terrace.

Beside the greenhouse our three dogwoods are like three bouquets of scarlet leaves. A cardinal lights in one and you wonder which is brighter, the foliage or the bird. Along comes a blue jay providing a contrast between his handsome blue and the handsome foliage.

This is the first time since August I have done anything on the terrace except pick flowers—which shows how carefree our garden actually is. Today I trimmed the ivy that grows in a luscious green ribbon along the house foundation hiding the cement and joining brick terrace floor to the upright boards of the house. The ivy squeezes up under the wooden uprights where it grows pale and skinny but none the less determined to get somewhere. Bob insists that if I don't cut it it will turn up in one of the bedrooms. There was that little plant that grew in our cellar long years ago. Somehow a small pot of ivy lay forgotten behind the workbench for a year, maybe longer. One spring I discovered it when poking amongst the junk that collects behind workbenches in cellars. The dirt in the pot was hard as a rock, the ivy, stark and dead except for one little pale white shoot with the most endearing new leaf unfurling at the tip. It appeared to be carved of ivory—a jewel in a pile of rags. I set the plant in the window. In due time with light and water it came to life and became quite a garden feature.

Never underestimate the power of an ivy, I thought as I looked at this today that was trying to push up under the house wallboards. But casting all romantic notions aside I briskly trimmed it back. When finished there was the attractive green ribbon of leaves, fifteen inches wide and forty feet long.

I have a special plan for winterizing the perennials this fall. I pulled up the dead marigolds, the low ones, and trimmed off the branches and laid them over the crowns of the delphiniums, milfoil, campanula, coral bells. On top of these branches I will spread leaves later on. Maple leaves tend to pack down and get soggy by spring, and sometimes they rot the plants beneath. But the stiff, wiry marigold stalks directly over the crown will prevent this.

The hoses were frozen and crackled slightly when I laid them in the sun to melt. I siphoned out the rain barrel so Bob could turn it upside down and wrap it in plastic for the months ahead. I pulled up the garden stakes. This is almost the last garden work of fall. Standing there in the golden sunlight with leaves swirling, I felt both a little prickle of happy anticipation for the winter and new season ahead and a touch of nostalgia for the season we are leaving.

There is something in us that doesn't ever want to let go to face even as inevitable a fact as a new season. Some people cling and cling like the oak leaves that hold on till next spring and the new ones push them off.

Last night flocks of wild geese flew over our house. In my half sleep I heard them honking. Unerringly they follow the rhythm of the seasons—their instinct telling them when to leave for southern climates. Some may not make the trip back and yet all go in good grace. Their great wide V stretches over the heavens, momentarily putting out the stars as they pass. When we human beings let go and embrace the new, when we flow with the seasons, and merge with the same basic rhythm that tells the geese when to go, we hear things beyond sound, and feel things beyond touch, and a kind of serenity settles over our spirits.

PART 5

Season of home and friends and family festivities

THE ROSES ARE COVERED, the garden a quiet area under its mulch of hay and leaves. Lawns are brown and the earth is cold and hard and unyielding to the touch. Nature has given her all and now goes her quiet independent way beneath the surface while we enjoy the sculptured shapes of leafless trees, bare stone walls, and rolling hillsides.

The garden world may not need us, but the birds do as they crowd the feeders every morning. A pair of bob-whites fly out of a gray sky to eat cracked corn two feet from our door with eager little cluckings. They are so tame we can almost touch them. Before they leave for their day's business they puff up and sit side by side for a while facing the sun, just touching each other.

These are the weeks of great cooking sessions, of new recipes and happy reunions of old friends. Children return from school and college, and holidays bring families together. Houses are gaily lit. Hearth fires crackle, and evergreens, fresh-gathered, bring in their cold and pungent fragrance as they decorate mantel and doorway.

At festive candle-lit parties we exchange a smile, a word, a thought. And through all the sharing of ideas and giving of gifts weaves a pattern of deepening relationships with those we love. An undercurrent of friendliness and warmth of spirit reaches beyond the tinsel-laden tree with its symbolic silver star at the top, beyond village and community to touch, in thought, other faraway members of the human family.

For yet another year Nature has guided people the world round through the seasons of preparation, of growth, and of harvest—and ushers us all now into the period of fulfillment.

II

November is yellow pumpkins and bittersweet

NOVEMBER IS CHILL, frosted mornings with a silver sun rising behind the trees, red cardinals at the feeders, and squirrels running scallops along the tops of the gray stone walls. A soft blue mist hovers against Pop's Mountain at dusk, and a white fur of frost lies along the clothesline when I hang out the sheets. The air is crisp and cold and last month's flaming foliage flames no more. November has its own colors, muted but equally appealing. Bare trees are gray, leaves ankle-deep in the woods are a rich brown, and hemlocks dark green. The water of our stream is black, the sumac seed-clusters maroon, and the stiff dead meadow grass straw-colored in the bright sun.

November is gray skies with gray clouds racing, a patch of blue, and a single shaft of sunlight piercing a jagged rift in the heavens. At the close of day sunsets of burnt orange or scarlet break through. Horizons broaden and the bones of the land show. The curving contours of our surrounding hills, hidden by foliage since last May, now stand revealed.

November can be wonderfully sunny days too, days of painting outdoors, of walking up the gorge, and of lunch on the terrace, but the moment the sun slips behind the hills the air has an ominous chill and you know that winter is close.

Nights are big and broad and full of stars. November stars aren't way off somewhere a million or so light years away but are tangled in the maple branches right over the house. They sparkle with a cold brilliance. If you could reach up above the bare treetops perhaps you could capture a handful. The pond along the lane is pricked at night with their lovely patterns.

We bring the star chart out of the cupboard and stand on the terrace greeting our old friends that we haven't thought about for months. Off to the east is Orion, and there Pegasus, and the neat little Pleiades, so close-knit a group. I am particularly fond of Delphinus, perhaps because of its name. Do I imagine the four stars that comprise it are rather blue? I often wonder what title our earth bears to beings perhaps poring over a star chart or something comparable on Venus, on one of the stars of Aries, or of Triangula. How self-centered we'd be if we believed that in all the cosmos we were the only existing civilization! There must be others, many other ways of life, and beings, even if their nature defies the imagination. Since this fact can be neither proved nor disproved I prefer to think it is true.

Now that leaves have fallen you not only see more stars by night but by day all sorts of exciting small items of beauty hitherto hidden. Here along the roadside is a tangle of violet-blue blackberry stems. Ranging streamers of bittersweet trail high from the top of a beech. Close to the gray stone walls wild red barberry fruit like Indian beads fringes spiny branches. Everywhere frosted goldenrod stalks are ashen—a sort of ghost flower now. And here an occasional oak seedling holds large leaves of coppery red, leaves that turn scarlet when the sun shines through.

Gray squirrels are busily packing away nuts for the winter. We all speculate—will it be a long snowy one or short and open—who knows? People love to ponder the signs. The woolly bear caterpillars are said to provide clues by their proportions of brown to black. Down by the mailbox yesterday I saw one all black! Whatever does this mean?

The cold earth is damp and chilly way down. When I go out to pull the carrots for dinner my fingertips tingle. One fine Sunday Bob digs up the carrots and beets and parsnips and buries them all in bushel baskets of sand set in the garage. Throughout the winter I will have the fun of reaching a hand down into the chilly sand and drawing out vegetables for dinner.

Some mornings a thin wafer of ice covers each bird feeder. When you are outdoors very long the wind and cold stiffen your face muscles; mittens are a must. How good the heated house feels when you come in. The same air that gave you a stuffy closed-in feeling last month, that seemed alien in October, becomes, all at once, a fine and welcome warmth.

This is the season of popcorn and milk for Sunday supper. On the back of the stove the melted butter waits, a bowl of gold, while the crackle of popping corn on the adjacent burner fills the air with lively sounds and a delicious fragrance. The snowy white puffed corn all but overflows the large cereal bowls, and, with salt and milk, makes a delicious meal.

Now that the trees are leafless we see and appreciate their various shapes. The shadblow rises gracefully from the edge of the north stone wall. The main trunk has a slight tilt which gives it a gay nonchalance. The branches are fine and numerous. How different the maple down by the brook. This staunch tree with its broad spread of sturdy limbs tells of cold and snow, icy winters, tender springs, lush green summers and passionate gold autumns. It speaks of the whole year's cycle and it stands for a kind of soundness that weathers every whim of nature. The spreading dogwood nearby still holds a few red leaves and its broadly reaching branches present quite a different aspect.

If trees might be likened to people the shadblow is a girl in her late teens, lithe and lovely, delicate and graceful. The maple is a solid matron, mother of five, who has known all sides of life and faces up to the challenges as well as to the joys and pronounces it all to be good. The elm is a gracious lady in a long chiffon evening dress, bowing to everyone but always with reserve and dignity. The oak is surely a Pilgrim Father and one who knows his own mind. A little rigid perhaps but sturdy and dependable.

This month all of a sudden we look at and see the *inside* of our house. In summer the furniture can need repair and the curtains attention, but it isn't until the cold weather that indoors receives its due. Just recently I began considering our vacuum cleaner which seemed a bit listless. I took it to be fixed, and succumbed to the charms and efficiency of a brand new one. It was lavender and white, and had a pull so strong that anything on the floor within three feet was in grave danger. How satisfying to see dust and scraps of paper inches away pulled in and swallowed up. The modern way is to have a paper bag for dust to accumulate in. You empty the bag without ever seeing or getting near its contents. This was my only disappointment. Personally I rather like that rich gray lumpy dirt that comes out of a vacuum. It gives you a sense of content to empty it and actually see what you're getting rid of. Now I'll be sanitary, I suppose, and modern, and efficient maybe, but I'm sure I shall miss taking a good look at the no longer needed items of our life that go out into oblivion in the vacuum innards.

One morning there was a perfectly terrible smell in Bob's bathroom. In fact we had to leave the window open and even this had no effect. For a week it grew steadily worse.

"Must be a dead rat," Bob said, "somewhere in the walls, no doubt." He sighed.

"Will we have to take down the wall, and which wall?" I asked.

When Mrs. Glover came over to see the new orchids there was quite a contrast between their fragrance and the odor at the other end of the house.

"Whatever will we do, Mrs. Glover?" I asked as we sat sipping peppermint tea.

She is always succinct. This time her response was one word.

"Wait."—A pause, then she added, "Takes 'bout three weeks."

We closed off the bathroom, used the other and kept the window open. Sure enough three weeks later all was well.

Mrs. Glover's peace of mind is tremendous. Perhaps I should say her acceptance. I never knew anyone who, without being spineless, so completely accepted what came—those things she could not alter. And with what wisdom did she adjust to them.

Tonight Bob is away on business. The wind is howling and the temperature has dropped. Every room in the house is a little chilly around the edges. The leaves are blowing across the brick terrace and against the house. The sound of their dry rustle comes in even through tight-shut windows. What a perfect evening to bake—and to make bread. Prowling through my recipes I came across one that I hadn't used lately. It needed to rise all night. The recipe was given to me by a wonderful large and black cook that my mother had years ago, just before Bob and I were married.

Katherine always had flour somewhere about her—on her apron, her hands, a smudge on her cheek or on her hair. She loved to bake and constantly made the most ambrosial bread, pies, cookies and cakes. It is no wonder that she weighed near 200 pounds. Had she been with us very many years we'd have probably approached 200 too!

Katherine taught me to make bread. On our wedding day her parting comment as Bob and I left for our honeymoon was: "See now that you keep the breadbox filled with homemade bread and you'll always have that man by your side. Keep the cookie jar filled for the chillun', and a few pies in the pantry and God will always bless your home."

Kneading dough provides some of the same contact with living things that working in a summer garden does. I like working with plants in all forms and all ways, and after all yeast is a plant too, and maintains a life of its own. There the dough lies on the wooden board beneath your hands, vital and slightly warm, and bouncy too. As you knead, the dough changes character. It starts out rather limp and spineless but rapidly develops a firm resiliency, a sort of independent existence. You feel the change occur through your finger tips.

The recipe for two loaves of graham bread that Katherine taught me is as follows:

Put 1 package of powdered yeast in 1/2 cup warm water (110°) and let stand 10 minutes.
Add 1/4 cup of molasses
2 rounded teaspoons salt
2 tbl. butter

Pour on this mixture 2 1/2 cups hot milk (110°). Stir.
Add 3 cups graham flour (organic), stir.
Add 4 cups of King Arthur unbleached flour (or 4 cups of mixed organic flours). Stir.
Knead on floured board for about 10 minutes. Smooth 1 tablespoon of oil over the surface. Set in a warm place. Let rise all night. In the morning cut down, let rise again in bread pans. Bake 45 minutes, placing in oven at 200° and resetting to 350°. This recipe makes a light bread that rises high.

A perfect breakfast for a chilly November morning is creamed eggs on toasted herb bread. My recipe for two loaves of herb bread, also light and high rising, is:

about 6 cups King Arthur white flour
(or 3 of whole wheat and 3 of white)
2 1/2 tsp. salt
2 tbl. soft butter
1/2 cup molasses (blackstrap makes a dark loaf, regular makes a lighter one. Honey can be substituted.)
1 cup old-fashioned slow-cooking rolled oats
2 cups boiling water
2 packages active dry yeast
1/3 cup lukewarm water
Let the yeast stand in warm water (temp. 110°) about 5 minutes. Soak rolled oats in boiling water 15 minutes. Mix yeast and all ingredients and add the herbs.
1/2 tsp. dried parsley
1 tsp. basil
1 tsp. anise seed
2 tsp. summer savory
1/4 tsp. thyme
Knead on floured board about 10 minutes. Cover and let rise in a warm place until double in bulk. Cut down and divide into well-greased pans. Let rise again but only until slightly rounded above the top of the pan. Set in oven at 200° and turn to 350°. Bake 45 minutes. It will rise further in the oven. Place on wire rack to cool, butter crust immediately. When cool store in plastic bag in icebox

or freezer. The fragrance of any bread baking is superb and this one simply cannot be described—it is that marvelous.

We live in a community of bread makers and a number of us are always sharing recipes and carrying on long phone conversations on the matter of proportions and countless other details. Bread was even the subject of the November meeting of the Fogs, Fairfield Organic Gardeners. Several of us demonstrated mixing and kneading. When we arrived, the house where the meeting was held was filled with the wonderful fragrance of baking bread.

Refreshments at the end of the afternoon were tea and slices of bread and butter with apple butter and jam. Every loaf had its recipe beside it. We tasted and tasted and copied out the rules we especially liked. Whole wheat, orange and nut, soy bread, and rye, light bread, solid bread, all sorts. Everyone went quite mad with the beautiful scent of hot rolls emerging from the oven and the flavor of all the different kinds. I couldn't eat any supper at all—and I doubt if anyone did!

Among other things that day I learned where pumpernickel first got its name. Many years ago in France Napoleon was presented by his chef with a new kind of bread. The Emperor said disdainfully that he didn't like it and added that it was "pain pour Nichole!" (bread for Nichole, his horse). Apparently however, Josephine and the rest of the household approved and the new bread caught on. Even Napoleon, they say, came around. And this is how we have the name and the bread today called pumpernickel!

By four o'clock the daylight is fading and by five lights are on. Every night we have candles at dinner and the soft golden flames add glamour to the meal as well as sending flickering shadows to the far corners. A burning candle, if you invite it to, stirs reflections, memories, and thoughts of the past. Candles are Christmas Eve and birthday cakes. A candle in a window on a dark night is comfort, cheer and welcome. I like to think how one candle lights another and loses none of its glow in the giving.

When I was a child we used to make clay candlesticks in school for our parents. Each one had a shield and a handle. I can well remember smoothing the clay under our art teacher's guidance. After it was fired I would tenderly bring it home to keep hidden until Christmas. Between my three sisters and myself, the house was filled with homemade candlesticks!

I can remember our Irish cook Delia going up the back stairs at night carrying a candlestick in one hand. There were gas jets in our house before we had electricity but the halls were dark and a candle was needed in the long, narrow, shadowy passages.

A few years ago my husband and I had an interesting experience in Italy. It had been a dreamy day. The climax came towards the end of it in an old church in an olive grove on the shores of Lago di Garda. We were in that dim quiet interior only a few minutes, but they were significant minutes.

This particular trip came after our children were grown and involved in their own lives. We were beginning a new phase of our marriage, and this vacation seemed a wonderful way to start. The little town of Sirmione was gay with summer tourists of all nationalities. There were almost too many people actually, and we escaped from the crowded narrow streets and headed for a little finger of land reaching out into the lake well beyond the town.

Leaving the last house we came to an olive grove. A small church stood in the center. The large double doors were invitingly open. At first we could see nothing but only feel the welcome coolness—a coolness almost like a caress after our warm walk. When our sight adjusted, the outlines of a gold altar emerged, racks of votive candles, and a woman in a black shawl kneeling on the stone floor before a figure of the Virgin. Stained glass windows, old paintings and statuary gradually came into view in the shadowed recesses and we noticed the subtle fragrance of incense.

After the press and rush of the small town it was pleasant to be alone in the little church except for one or two shadowy figures. We paused before a group of burning candles. On sudden impulse I whispered to my husband, "Let's light a candle to us and our marriage."

He, in response, dropped a coin in a box and picked up a tall slim white candle and handed it to me. I lit it from one of those others already burning and together we set it in a little rack beside a dozen or more brightly glowing.

Standing there my thoughts reached back beyond these holiday weeks. In any home with three children to raise things happen—things not only rewarding and wonderful but things that are difficult too. Some way we had worked through them, finding always that it isn't enough to sit and let things happen. Whether they are good or bad you must, at times, take definite action. There in that little church in the olive grove in Italy the memory of certain high points and joys filled me with thanksgiving. The brightly burning flame became a response, a symbol, and an assurance of continuous unfolding and richness in this new phase of life ahead.

For a moment we stood watching our candle burn, and all at once the flame paled, turned blue, and flickered uncertainly. Sudden panic seized me. Before I could say a word, Bob reached out, picked it up just before it went out, and relit it from the next one. With a sigh of relief I watched the candle come to life again.

The square of sunlight at the church door beckoned but we could not go until we were sure our candle would burn with a bright clear flame. To my horror once again it dimmed. This time when my husband picked it up he studied it a moment. Then he tipped out quite a lot of surplus liquid wax that was snuffing the flame.

"Of course," he said thoughtfully, "you have to work at it, do something about it to keep it burning brightly." He spoke gently and in a low voice, more to himself than to me. He set the candle back with the others. This time it had really caught and burned a deep golden yellow. We waited a few moments just to be sure all was well, then stepped out into the brilliant sun.

Betty's words made me sad.

"We simply don't have a thing in common any more," she was saying, "we think differently on every subject, and are seriously considering parting—there seems no other way."

Betty and I were having tea by the fire on a rainy afternoon. She rushed on. "When the children were home we were too busy to realize how much Stan and I were growing apart, but now it is very evident."

It seemed to relieve her to talk so I listened, and refilled her cup occasionally. As she talked on, elaborating their differences, I was reminded of a time when we had been married a number of years and I was telling a wise friend of mine how I wished Bob could only think as I did about a certain situation. She said nothing for a moment, then asked,

"Are you, by any chance, saying that you wish your husband thought like a woman?"

This set me back where I belonged quite firmly.

It *is* a challenging phase of marriage, when the last child takes off and you are alone with your husband for the first time in so many years. Much has changed. You've grown, you hope, but in the process both of you may have developed points of view that differ. Now all at once you face these differences. Two people who have been through trying and triumphant experiences together, in certain respects, may suddenly feel strangers.

Divorce may sometimes seem the only answer, but surely it is to be avoided if at all possible.

Occasionally, if two people just hang on willy nilly until a storm passes and then take stock, they find they have passed by the obstructions, and grown considerably in the process without even knowing it. If they can laugh about this afterwards they are doubly blessed.

Marriage is too vast a subject to try and say in a sentence exactly what it is about. Mary Webb says, "Love is a lot of colored threads, and one master thread of pure gold." Love and marriage seem to me to be a good deal about growing, and a growing that involves not only the joy and excitement inherent in all change and newness, but also a kind of coping.

Young people are so often attracted by their very differences. Two people may never think of it at the time they are first drawn together but, in these opposing traits each has something the other needs for growth and balance. The requirement is to accept the healthiness of these variations and understand their potential. Then what might have been a parting point becomes a cornerstone of something new and rich.

Where there are differences things happen, good things, and growth occurs. All around us in nature and in man's world we see evidences of this. Different levels of land form a stream bed where water flows and fresh energy is generated. The contrast of dry heat and moisture combine to waken and stir the germ of life in a seed. Positive and negative electricity bring about a potential for work, and new things come into being.

Where there are contrasts in a marriage relationship we tend to single out one way or the other as being right, rather than appreciating the beauty of the difference, and the wonder of the interaction that ensues. It is this coming together of two opposing forces that leads to a new whole greater than its components. In the merging of the variations and their interaction upon each other we have invited a fresh and exciting third way. In this blend we touch the "master thread of pure gold."

Bob and I sometimes stumble over one basic difference. Bob steps hesitatingly into the water of certain new experiences, first with one toe, then with one foot. On the other hand I leap in and nearly drown. Obviously a middle road is needed. I feel impatient with his hesitation and he feels pushed by my rush. When we can get together on entering a new experience by my husband stretching forward, and by my holding back, the new way, neither his nor mine but the third way that we have built together, proves to be the best of all.

Occasionally when we stub our toes on some difference we can laugh. Sometimes we sputter and mutter. Once in a while we have a battle. A few hours later there we are the same two people we were before the disagreement. The bird feeders need filling, the suet stick is empty, and dinner needs preparing. The roof leak must be repaired and Bob is soon up there with a can of tar. In moments of stress how much steadying lies in the support of familiar activities that compose a day. These so often shake some of the ornery human nonsense out of us.

"Come on," says Bob after a while, "let's walk up Wells Hill and see the view now that the leaves are off."

The battle really didn't cause fatal damage. Something was there underneath, as there is in almost all marriages. Something that could take it and stand firm. It is a kind of a warp and woof that can support practically any kind of pattern woven into it.

A walk in the woods these days is a treasure hunt. November is the season of terrariums. Such choice jewels we discover—a tiny cluster of red-tipped lichen, a choice tangle of gray reindeer moss, a light green group of miniature fairy cups. And here a small four-inch hemlock, and a tiny one-inch fern. If we forget the basket and trowel we have to dig in the cold earth with our fingers, and come home with treasures tied in Bob's handkerchief and my beret.

On Sunday Joan came down alone. The boys were off on a week-end with friends. We celebrated her birthday. After presents and cake and candles we took to the woods—this time with baskets. When we could carry no more we turned home to settle on the floor of the greenhouse with all available glass containers. Giant brandy breathers are the loveliest with their graceful shapes. Old aquariums, any kind of fish bowls and even tall goblets will do. Each container needs a cover—plastic preferred, but lacking that glass cut to fit or Saran wrap suffices.

My favorite way to make a terrarium is to select a piece of the soft moss that grows like a blanket over old stumps and rocks. With the green side out you can line the glass. Root small ferns and plants in leaf mold on top of this upside-down moss. The terrariums I like the best have a hill and a vale, a depth and a height. The hill is made of a fat cushion of moss. Until I go terrarium hunting I always forget about the many different kinds of enchanting moss, and what a beautiful contrast they make in the same bowl. There is short-haired Kelly-green moss, long-haired moss, gray-green moss, red-tipped moss. I tuck in small pieces of all these around tiny plants and ferns, using a pair of long-handled tweezers. For added charm keep the sense of a curving path running through the terrarium. Plant the taller material on one side. A focal point of interest can be an unusual bit of lichen-covered rock or bark.

One thing I am adamant about—in a terrarium there must be nothing artificial, no dyed pebbles, little Japanese figures, bridges, nothing that stems from the hand of man. A perfect terrarium to me is a microcosm, a natural woods, or unadulterated forest in miniature. As such it brings pure magic to the room where it stands.

A terrarium does best with one side of its glass touching a north window pane. It will also thrive on a table in the center of the room—the cooler the room the better. Keep away from sun lest a mold start inside the glass. Once a day lift the top off a few minutes for air. If you breathe into it you feed it carbon dioxide. A light sprinkle of water inside every week is all the care needed. A terrarium lasts indoors weeks, months, and often until spring.

Mary and I ate sandwiches in the rain forest that day! It was sunny and bright as I drove down the Merritt Parkway. Streamers of bittersweet festooned the trees, sheafs of scarlet berries on the black alders caught the sun, on both sides of the highway. I had told Mary I would pick her up at 9:30. After a few minutes in her greenhouse seeing what had grown since I'd last been there we ventured forth.

First we visited our friend Rodney Wilcox Jones, the well-known orchid grower. He raises orchids as a hobby in a number of greenhouses in back of his house in New Rochelle. Rodney has what appears to be a nonchalant way of caring for them all, but as you listen and watch him handle his plants you realize that he knows each one thoroughly, and meticulously meets its needs.

He and his wife greeted us warmly. They were opening a newly arrived parcel post package.

"Here's our parachute—just in time," exclaimed Charlotte enthusiastically, as she drew out yards of white nylon material and 600 feet of line!

Orchids have led us into many new and exotic worlds, but never before to parachutes! Mary and I exchanged glances.

"We use it to cover the overhead glass in the conservatory," said Rodney, "it lets the light in and is circular like the ceiling, and much better looking than whitewash."

"It just came in time for our Thanksgiving party, and I'm going to weave the extra line into a rug," Mrs. Jones added gathering it all up carefully.

After we had encompassed the parachute and written down the address of where to buy one just in case—we went out to the greenhouses. Orchids were trailing down from the roof, hanging off the walls, springing to life even under the benches—and of course the benches themselves were burgeoning. Each different house had its special varieties and temperature. We were excited with the beauty of them all—from great Cattleyas with their ruffled petals and swirling patterns to the tiniest Lockhartia the size of a small fly! And we were pleased to see Rodney's new cross that he proudly showed—a rich tawny red orchid. Our host's enthusiasm was contagious. He has such affection for each plant, and you know this as you watch him.

An hour or so later we left, our heads swimming with new ideas and facts of culture, and our arms loaded with new plants. We arrived at the Botanical Garden at lunch time.

"Let's eat in the rain forest," said Mary.

From a cold November day we stepped into a hot and steaming jungle. We found a low stone wall and sat between Psilotum nudum, and Syngonium macrophyllum—both from Central America. They were lovely in spite of their names. Almost hidden behind a curtain of great long trailing roots that swung down from the upper limbs of various tropical trees we ate our sandwiches and Joan's leftover birthday sponge cake. Beside us a lush and turgid stream was blanketed with bright green algae. The air was so humid and relaxingly warm that pretty soon we didn't want to move or even think coherently. Everything beyond our present line of vision seemed completely unimportant. The begonias in the shadows, the orchids trailing on the branches, the exotic red powder puff tree, Calliandra, were all intriguing.

After wandering a while among the ferns, and feeling their foliage so soft and pleasant I said, "Mary, if we don't leave now we never will!"

Just in time we escaped to the orchid propagating houses to see and study all the different varieties. You learn so much from asking questions, and observing how others handle the same plants you grow. We also marvelled at the many orchids that were totally unfamiliar. There is so much to absorb about these fascinating plants—will I ever master half of it!

Joan and the children arrived Thanksgiving morning. Almost before we heard the car the two boys were rushing into the house bringing their special kind of vigor.

"Here are the newest marbles I've just fried and frosted," Jeff burst out in a quick breath drawing out of his pocket a handful like colored ice crystals—beautiful, really.

"Grandpa," interrupted Jesse, "did you know that the

Amazon River is 150 miles wide at the mouth—the delta, and that there are one million square miles of rubber trees in Brazil?"

"And the Pilgrims"—Jeff plunged on—"did you know that—"

They both talk fast, and are jumping up and down at the same time. Plunk go the suitcases—and quickly they have their clothes changed. Presently Joan and all of us are outdoors winterizing the roses. A little ten-inch-high mound of compost goes in the center of each one and while Bob and the boys are getting this Joan and I are pruning the plants. Jesse and Jeff never walk, they run. One has the dump cart, the other the wheelbarrow and they bring the compost almost faster than Bob can pile it on each plant. Hay and leaves to cover the tops of the canes are there in a jiffy. The bed is fenced in with chicken wire to hold everything in place. While in the mood we cover the perennials also, and on top of leaves lay hemlock boughs, trimmed from the trees in the north meadow.

While we catch our breath the boys begin pitching horseshoes, and this is soon followed by badminton. Jesse winds up until Bob tells him he looks like a pretzel as he hits the bird. Both seem to be as much in the air as on the ground when they reach high or stoop low to return a shot.

The great project of the day, however, is yet to come. A tall elm along the north wall is to be felled. Bob and the boys carry out the electric saw and the yards of black cable. The whine of the saw soon fills the crisp sunny air. This tree has supported many oriole nests since we have lived here, and I'm sure it has swung its foliage in summer breezes for a goodly number of years before that. For two seasons now it has stood dead, and an attractive silvery gray color. But it must come down lest it blow over in a storm and do damage. Jesse and Jeff stand watching the power saw eat a great wedge out of the trunk. Bob plans to fell it between a cedar and a small maple. The space is scarcely wider than the elm trunk itself.

Can he possibly do this? The sawdust scatters its fragrant golden specks over the dead grass. The boys stand hypnotized, the saw whines—the wedge grows. Joan and I go out when the final moment approaches. Jesse and Jeff, one on each end of the great cross-cut saw, do the last cutting by hand.

We hear a little sharp crack.

"Timber," Bob calls and he and the boys step rapidly aside. The top sways slightly, then moves faster and faster and finally down comes the great tree. With a couple of bounces on the ground it scatters small branches and twigs every which way before it settles in a final heap. The elm fell precisely between the cedar and the maple, and everyone is pleased. Now that small maple, free and clear, will grow and develop and one day replace the elm.

Joan and I leave the woodsmen and take to the kitchen where the turkey has scented the whole house. The table is gay with last month's autumn leaves from the freezer. They have held their color magnificently—and are bright as the cranberry sauce that stands among them. No more welcome smell exists this month than that of a New England Thanksgiving dinner—not only the turkey, but onions, mashed potatoes, gravy, squash, mince pie, pumpkin pie. All the fragrances mingle into an aroma beyond compare.

When the children and Joan have left, when the last dish is in place and the table made small again—for two instead of five—the house is dead quiet. We ourselves have become lost in the silence. We sit by the fire that has burned down to pure red embers now, each of us with a book. We are comfortably tired, and how very content, as always after a good family get-together. I begin thinking of our children in the West—and wondering how they are, and visualize the grandchildren and their family time, and my sisters and their families too—and then thoughts of good friends pass through my mind. I begin musing on Thanksgiving and how much there is to appreciate all year long as well as on this day.

Of course, family and friends and interesting work—

people to love, and people who love us; love to give, and love to receive, these are the familiar and basic ingredients of a good life. If we have these we are indeed blessed.

Across the room Bob is deep in his book. The embers glow. Certain particular scenes and pictures lifted from the whole year now pleasantly drift one by one across my inner vision, blotting out the page of the book before me. In recollection each memory brings some special sense of joy and contentment.

I am thankful for light—all kinds, man-made and natural. How lovely is dawn light, starlight, sunlight on green grass, candlelight, house lights on stormy nights, or on any night, street lights, and firelight.

There is the magic of shining car lights on wet pavements on rainy nights. The mysterious lights on bridges like necklaces of diamonds in the gloaming. I am thinking of the George Washington bridge in New York City when first lit at dusk. One of my favorite lights is the yellow beam of our outside light that greets us from down the road when we have been away for the evening.

Aside from lights I am glad to be living in a world where there are butter-yellow dandelions to star green lawns spring and fall; dandelion seed puffs, mere whiffs of down blowing through the air; the courting song of the Baltimore oriole; the turn of a season, any season; the free shining hair of little girls in the sun on summer beaches; the touch of sun-warmed earth when planting seeds; rows of tiny seedlings in May; the cool firm feel of orange carrots pulled from a summer earth; rain and rainbows; reflections in puddles that sometimes turn the common scene, perhaps a very ordinary house and telegraph pole, to a painting by an old Dutch master. And the first streaming sunlight after a week of gray days and showers.

In my mind I see again the view of blue lakes, woods, and a single white church spire from a nearby hilltop; soft green moss in the forest. I smell the scent of a wet wood pile after a shower; the first whiff of outdoors when you have been indoors with a cold a few days. How pleasant is a blue china pitcher filled with milk; thick yellow cream, the smell of fresh sweet butter, and the smoothness of a hen's egg. I especially like green strawberry leaves with white rims of early morning frost and the brilliant green of parsley in October; a small johnny-jump-up blooming in the gravel drive in February; the graceful curve of a snowdrift outside the window.

Such a list is quite without end. Letting the pictures come is a pleasant pastime at any season. Once you begin highlighting scenes and moments of richness and joy they grow and multiply and come to you from all years and all seasons. It is surprising how many little daily things include themselves. Perhaps these are more important than we consider them to be.

Man and his foibles, his failures and his triumphs will come and go as will what he devises and creates. But much that is around him, the simple natural world he lives in will endure always. There will always be moss in the forest, and birds, views from hilltops, seeds to sprout, harvests to gather in, seasons that change, rain that falls in silver streaks, rainbows and a sliver of new moon with a star up close. And there will always be man's opportunity and privilege of participating to some extent in all of these things, the cycles of nature, the seasonal changes, the planting, growing, harvesting, and all the rest.

This is perhaps the thing above all else to thank God for.

12

December is hearth fires, home, and holidays

THE DECEMBER SUN rises silver behind leafless trees. Sparkling like a great cold jewel, it hangs suspended over the eastern hills. Long slanting rays stream through the branches, gradually turning the meadow from white back to golden brown as the fur of morning frost disappears. The mist in the valley is blue, sunsets are golden, fields and woods are brown. Freckled sycamore trunks stand out in the bare forests with ash-white limbs twisting upward and outward. Bright green Christmas ferns, each pinna shaped like a long holiday stocking, toe and all, scramble helter skelter over the rich coppery colored leaves on the ground.

By four o'clock the light begins to fade, and twilight comes fast. Each morning the temperature hovers around 18°. This is the month when we wonder where our little shrew lives. Yesterday we saw him skitter around the corner of the garage and disappear inside. We never find him in the summer, but this time of year he appears. Can he be nesting in the old pile of burlap bags in that forgotten corner or behind the car tires? I hope he doesn't discover the new orchid potting fiber!

Our terrace is alive with birds. Cardinals, titmice, chickadees, juncos, woodpeckers and nuthatches are regular visitors. They all welcome suet along with seed and crumbled stale breadcrusts. As they dart and fly this way and that they trace a sort of invisible pattern through the air. If you imagined each bird trailing a single gossamer thread in a different rainbow color what a skein of tangled beauty they would all weave together!

The black water of the Saugatuck flows slowly, the edges fringed with ice. Down the lane the pond is frozen and we get our skates out of the attic to be sharpened. When we walk up towards the reservoir the rush of water through the gorge has a chill and icy sound, and it is an invigorating fresh cold air that we breath in.

Some days it rains and ice gathers on the windshield and paved roads freeze glassy. How glad we are to turn in the drive on such an afternoon, draw the car into the garage, carry the shopping packages into the house and just be home. And then the first snow comes. Step outside and the flakes touch your face with little pricks of cold. A snowflake, it seems, when up high and first born is a solid particle, a droplet of cloud moisture. Then miraculously, it grows. Three such particles may adhere together, the larger crystal take over. In the growing the beautiful hexagonal shapes and intricate details of design develop, and no two snowflakes ever come out the same.

"Don't make plans for the week-end," Bob said on Monday.

"Why?" I asked. It would be our wedding anniversary and the fortieth.

"Oh, I have ideas," my husband replied mysteriously, "and I don't believe I will tell you."

So there it was, and secretly I was glad that no coaxing could get anything out of him.

Saturday morning Bob said to pack my suitcase with city clothes. How novel and pleasant to pack for you don't know exactly what or where, and to be completely in someone else's hands. At four-thirty we started off and I still didn't know our destination.

We headed for the Tappan Zee bridge over the Hudson.

"Oh, we must be going to see Fran and Mark in New Jersey."

"Do you think so?" asked Bob, secretive to the end. Soon we turned back towards New York City. My husband was enjoying his success in utterly confusing me.

A half hour later we were in the Harvard Club, installed in a delightful room decorated in Harvard colors. A great dignity permeated the solid dark furniture, red rug, and curtains. We ate a fabulous dinner in the large high-ceilinged dining room with all the past Harvard presidents looking down from the walls. Dinners there are buffet and you pick and choose and want everything—lobster, roast beef, handsome and heavenly salads, pumpkin pie. How can you resist—you don't even try!

It was rather exciting not to know where we were going for the evening. When we settled in a taxi I listened with interest to the directions Bob gave the driver. So—we were to see Lillian Gish in *Anya,* the story of Anastasia of Russia and a gay and interesting play it turned out to be. Afterwards we walked down Fifth Avenue admiring the Christmas decorations and the tall spectacular Rockefeller Center tree.

Sunday morning we heard a fine talk by Dr. Seale at Philharmonic Hall. He said that Jefferson and the great people of the world have one trait in common. They give their all to the situation of the moment. In so doing everything else falls into second place to be dealt with effectively when its time is due.

Be definite, be decisive, Dr. Seale emphasized, and give the business at hand your best. I am always glad to be reminded of the importance and rewards of being completely with the current activity whether it is getting dinner, listening to a symphony or talking to a friend. The human mind, especially mine, if let, can be such a vagrant wanderer!

Driving home Sunday afternoon I felt I had been away a week! We had done so much and had such a marvelous time —and the pleasantest aspect of all was the complete surprise.

I can only call it the Miracle of the Jade Tree. Last month while we were admiring Mr. Jones' orchids he picked up a can of general insecticide and sprayed some mealy bugs comfortably nestled on the underside of a leaf.

"I didn't know you could use *that* on orchids," I said in amazement. "Won't it kill the plant?"

"Never has," Rodney said squirting another cluster of white cotton half hidden under a sheath. Immediately I remembered our jade tree and our struggle with these creatures. The organic gardener in me shrank from using poison spray for any purpose whatever but the mealy bug situation broke down my resistance.

Nearly every branch needed a squirt. Next morning not a mealy bug was visible. BUT two days later all the sprayed leaves began turning black and drying up. In the next few days they wrinkled and curled into a deplorable state, and our beloved tree, cherished these many years, seemed about to die.

A couple of Mays ago we had put it outdoors and it got frosted. Half the leaves fell then yet miraculously it survived. I had the fond hope that something similar might happen this time. But every day the floor was showered with newly fallen leaves. Sitting nearby you could actually hear them drop. For about two weeks this went on. All of a sudden one morning as I was picking up dead leaves, I noticed on one denuded branch tip infinitesimal pinheads of new growth. Sure enough, on examining the tree little leaflets in pairs, dewdrop size, could be seen everywhere that others had died and fallen. These fresh young buds of new green are as exciting as the great amaryllis flower in the greenhouse.

And here in the amaryllis lies a miracle of another sort. I received two bulbs in October and followed directions about sun and watering. After several weeks four great buds began unfolding in one pot. Surprisingly enough they were only just above the rim. Each dazzling orange-red blossom grew to eight inches across when fully opened. No one who saw them could believe they were real. These huge flowers dominated the greenhouse and the dining table where we put them each night. After the first four blossoms faded another stalk rose supporting four more equally large. A look in the heart of one of these blossoms leaves you speechless.

Which is more stirring, the amaryllis or the little new leaves on the jade tree? In both great and dramatic blossom and in tiny beginnings of new growth you sense something beyond and greater than either jade tree or amaryllis. Yet it is they that evoke the broader vision.

In a cloud of steam and a burst of drama the washing machine breathed its last. Tony who faithfully repairs our utilities had told me some weeks before when replacing a part that the machine had just about had it.

"What can you expect after fifteen years?" he asked. "Next time you have trouble perhaps you had better consider a new one. I can go on fixing this for some time, of course, but it keeps on costing you, and I'd like to see you with a brand new one."

That day the washer was filled with sheets and suds and was bowling along merrily. I was kneading bread in the kitchen nearby when all at once I heard a subtle sound, odd and not quite normal. But before I sensed trouble there came a loud whish and water began pouring out the bottom of the washing machine in a mad stream that engulfed the baskets of apples and vegetables on the floor nearby. Before I could get myself out of the bread, water began swirling into the kitchen, circling under the icebox and heading for the dining room. It was so hot that the rising steam created the atmosphere of a sauna!

After whirling the dial through several cycles hopefully but to no avail I thought of turning off the water. Immediately everything came to a groaning halt, but the washing machine, still full of water and sheets kept right on emptying itself. It was increasing the humidity if nothing else, I thought, mopping, swishing, and sweeping.

In due time everything was reasonably serene and Tony said he would be there in an hour. I began thinking about a new washing machine.

On Saturday Bob and I went to Sears Roebuck and bought one that is so intelligent that it can do practically everything except cook the meals! We turned down one with a rainbow of buttons because it really was *too* sophisticated. Press one button and the machine gives a nylon slip the proper water temperature, number of soapings and rinsings calculated to bring health and longevity to a nylon slip. Ditto for sheets, shirts, socks and so forth. With this I might altogether lose the ability to evaluate and make decisions. The one we chose is pretty remarkable, however. Perhaps the most fun is watching a colored washcloth drawn down under the suds in some mysterious manner. All the clothes move from up to down and back up again as well as agitating from side to side.

A hardware store draws Bob as a magnet draws a nail!

And my husband soon disappeared in that department of Sears to wander dreamily among the saws, hammers, screws and countless other fascinating items. A few minutes later he reappeared.

"Look, I have just bought a soldering gun and a mitre box for Jesse and Jeffrey for Christmas. Come on, let's cross the street and get some coffee in the donut shop."

Never before have I seen so many choices in donuts. Here Heinz' 57 Varieties had met their equal. You could have donuts flavored with apple, raspberry, pineapple, cherry, blueberry, cinnamon, peach, apricot and on and on.

My New England husband said, "I'll have one plain donut please—no, not risen."

I couldn't make up my mind but finally settled on a risen cherry. It was sensational, immense and very inorganic!

The garden is completely winterized except for the roses which need more hay and the four small box yet to be covered with burlap. We have a sentimental feeling for these box. Once many years ago on a holiday with the children we were driving to North Carolina. We stopped in Mt. Vernon and bought four seedlings, cuttings of George Washington's original box hedge. They were twenty-five cents each, and now they are nearly two feet tall. Every fall Bob builds a little covered patio of burlap around each one.

After telephoning here and there I located hay for mulching that we organic gardeners covet for roses. Mr. Eldredge's farm was a few miles off in an area of fields and cows. He himself turned out to be an earthy character wearing an old sweater and appropriately weathered dungarees. After fitting the bales into the back of the car he asked hopefully and with a gleam in his eye if I didn't want to go in and see his cows that were cheerfully chewing their cuds in the barn beside us. I happen to like cows and the man seemed so eager that I said I'd love to.

Mr. Eldredge led the way with the same joy and pride I

feel when I take people around our place. I guess those cows were his garden. His forty black and white Holsteins, to my delight, still had their horns. In Switzerland the cows all have horns and we were told that the horn, reaching up towards heaven, draws some kind of mysterious cosmic energy out of the air and conveys this to the milk, and that therefore milk from horned cows has more food value. I must say Swiss cheese, milk and chocolate do taste rather special. I didn't think Mr. Eldredge would be receptive to the cosmic energy idea though, so I didn't mention it. He proceeded through aisles of cows, stretching out a hand here and there to scratch a head or pat a flank. We came to a pen of very young calves. How wonderful are the eyes of a newborn calf with their melting softness and look of trust.

On this pleasant tour I noticed off in a corner a great bathtub filled with bread crusts. What a shock to learn that they pick up stale bakery bread from the vicinity for the cows. The combination of being an organic gardener and a bread maker has led me, whether justifiably or not, to the conclusion that ordinary white store bread doesn't have much good in it.

Obviously it would never do to question this while my host was telling me that *all* the farms nowadays fed their cows stale bread for protein.

A barn filled with cows is a comfortable place. A yellow cat lay curled on a pile of hay and another with four small kittens rose up out of the shadows and set off a series of tiny mews. Mr. Eldredge picked up a young kitten that was playing beside a cow's hoof and carried it with us in the crook of his arm.

Cows and hay and kittens are a basic part of the country and I do enjoy living where a few miles' drive brings you to them all.

Next day I spread hay on the roses to insulate them against our cold New England winds and weather. Spoiled hay is as pleasant and fragrant as regular hay. It just got rained on at the wrong time and they can't feed it to the cows.

As I snugged large armfuls around each bush I moved in an aura of hay scent. In just three months more, I thought, we'll be uncovering these same bushes and marvelling at tiny red swellings along the stalks, swellings that soon emerge into leaves and flowers. Over towards the perennial bed topped with hay and hemlock boughs I could also visualize the blue delphinium in all its glory and the great Auratum lily. But I drew my thoughts back to December and to hay and roses because these months before spring have their own richness and besides I was enjoying what I was doing, and wanted to be with it.

While I was laying the last of the hay over the plants I heard a crackling of underbrush and up the bank from the brook bounded a deer and two nearly grown fawns. All three stopped and stood looking about the meadow. I froze where I was, hoping to resemble a haystack. What a beautiful sight they were, those three wild creatures. After a few moments they turned and loped back down the bank, and the crackling of brush gradually subsided. These surprise glimpses of the deer that we know live all through our surrounding forests are among the cherished moments of our year.

Looking up herb butter in Adele Davis' cook book led me to new culinary delights. An ordinary steak becomes ambrosia when spread with herb butter before broiling. This is how you make it:

Combine:
1/4 lb. (1/2) soft butter or margarine
1 tbl. dried parsley
1 tbl. minced or dried chives
1/2 tsp. each savory, marjoram, basil, tarragon
1 minced clove garlic
1/4 tsp. paprika

Blend well and pack into a small covered jar. Keep in the refrigerator.

Herb butter is excellent on lamb chops, leg of lamb, roast beef, hamburgers, roast turkey, broiled chicken, and pork chops. And also delectable on baked potatoes.

Another wonderful recipe came into our lives the day I fell heir to a book about the Hunzas. The Hunzas are the race who live in the heart of the Himalayas and in a rather remarkable state of health and longevity. Various doctors and scientists have studied these people to try to learn how and why they live to be a hundred and forty-five years old! At this great age they are still hale and hearty, singing, dancing, planting, harvesting, and climbing mountains. It seems that one cause of their bounding health and vigor is that the mountain streams in their land run milky white with minerals. The earth is equally rich in health-giving properties. Hunza land is said to be the place from which years ago James Hilton's *Lost Horizon* was drawn.

In my Hunza book I discovered chapattis. Chapattis resemble slightly, in looks and flavor, the tortillas of Guatemala and Mexico. They take only a few minutes to make and are absolutely delicious. For two people measure a cup of freshly ground whole wheat flour (organic if possible), 1/4 tsp. salt. Mix in with finger tips 1/8 lb. butter or margarine. Add 1/4 cup water—a little more if necessary. Knead together, cover with a damp cloth and leave for thirty minutes. With a floured rolling pin, roll out round shapes whatever size you like and very thin. I make ours about three inches in diameter. Cook on a greased griddle, and if electric set at 360°. Let one side cook until lightly brown, turn and let the other side brown. Serve with sweet butter for dinner in the place of bread. They are unique, utterly delicious and best when served piping hot from griddle to butter plate. Eat immediately.

Once, driving west, we stopped beside a field of ripe wheat because it was so beautiful. A fellow traveller also stood admiring the golden crop. He turned out to be a retired wheat farmer and he showed us how to roll a head of grain in the palm of the hand and blow off the chaff. Eating those wheat grains right there beside the field where they had grown was quite an experience. They had a nutty taste and must have abounded in pure unadulterated wheat germ. The Hunza chapattis have the same delicious and distinctive flavor.

I read that the Hunzas travel about with a bag of grain and a grinder. When they stop for a meal they fresh-grind wheat flour and there by the roadside make a fire and cook chapattis for lunch, dinner, or breakfast as the occasion demands. Eat a few of these and you have eaten something that stays by you. The fresh-ground whole wheat flour also contains trace elements, so as well as being excellent in flavor, chapattis are high in food value.

When I go to buy orchids in a commercial greenhouse I am inclined to lose my head and get far more than intended. Here I was walking among hundreds of Cattleyas and I could have as many as I wanted, all entirely free. I was out of my mind with excitement.

I had called Mr. Henderson to ask about repotting some orchids bought from him a number of weeks before. He was moving to Florida and had been selling everything off.

"Have you disposed of all the orchids?" I asked.

"No, but I'm not going to turn the greenhouse heat on tonight, so those that remain will freeze. Could you use more—you're welcome to them."

I said I'd be right over and immediately called Mary.

"Certainly, get some for me—about five." she said.

I thought I could perhaps squeeze in a half dozen—but no more.

When I arrived there were several other amateur orchid growers there selecting plants. Orchid people are just naturally friendly. When these men had filled their own cars they began picking out the best of the remaining plants and carrying them out for me. None of us could bear to think of all these orchids freezing up tonight. We considered ourselves the rescue squad!

By now my resistance completely dissolved. I watched the back car seat fill, the front seat, the floor back and front. I had barely room to sit before the wheel when one of my new friends appeared bearing a large Cattleya with seven buds.

"You have to take this one," he balanced it on top of some others. "Can't let it freeze."

I drove home at fifteen miles an hour lest I dislodge something. The greenhouse was filled to the eyebrows—no room even to step inside. I counted thirty-five new ones. Certainly Bob will have comments tonight, I thought—and he did. Mainly he was amused and actually impressed by our windfall of beautiful healthy plants. Next day Elsie came to clean and became deliriously happy at the thought of taking home a real live orchid plant in bud. Mary also came and we divided them and each had seventeen new ones.

These days the car is always filled with Christmas presents on the way in or the way out. One time we were in New York City with presents to deliver and we parked our convertible. When we returned the presents were gone and the top neatly slit with a little triangle just large enough to reach in and draw things out. The gifts did look rather festive in their gay paper and ribbons. I've often considered though, what their effect was on the person who appropriated them. He overlooked a suitcase and overcoat in the back seat, and took instead a package of wild bird food destined for my brother-in-law and a book called *The Power of Constructive Thinking* by Emmet Fox. I've never ceased to wonder about the reaction of this particular thief as he opened his haul.

Today I learned how to turn *Reader's Digests* into angels, pipe cleaners into halos and artichokes into Christmas decorations! It began with the rug-hooking group at Florence Price's. Garret was in his studio finishing up a *New Yorker* illustration, but came out to join us from time to time. In one of his forays into the feminine world he brought a large flower pot full of grass. Every fall he pots up an ordinary piece of sod—his winter houseplant, he says, and it is lovely. The vivid green grass on that rainy cold bleak day changed the whole character of his studio.

"Ferns—everyone has ferns," Garret said, "but how few think to grow grass indoors." His grass garden was about eight inches high and he was just about to trim it.

"Such a contrast to mowing the lawn," he laughed. "Just two or three snips with the scissors."

One of the members of the rug-hooking group came in with an armful of angels.

"They're all made from *Reader's Digests*," she announced. "You only need a four-cent dowel stick, silver and gold paint, and a few glitters. Come on, I'll show you how."

You fold each page from the top outer corner into the center crease and flatten the fold with your finger. Part of the outer page edge now lies horizontal across the page. Next, the bottom outer corner is folded up to meet this horizontal page edge. Run through the whole magazine doing this. About an hour later you end up with a perky stiff shape that flares outward, forms a complete circle and stands alone. Slide the dowel stick down the center hole. The angel's head, a styrofoam ball tennis-ball-size, goes on the extended top of this. Bits of glitter stuck in with pins become eyes, nose and mouth. Lipstick adds rosy cheeks. A few inches of curtain fringe pinned on makes a jaunty little cap and neck ruff. From aluminum foil cut wings and glue between the pages at each side. Three large silver paper buttons may be cut to go down the front. A colored pipe cleaner bent into a circle forms the final touch—the halo!

Every year I always seem to be spraying something with gold paint. Last Christmas I was gilding a hoe. Bob and I were going to a New Year's Eve party and were invited to dress as our hidden selves. Bob as a gentleman farmer wore a tux and carried a few garden tools, the metal parts gilded for the occasion. One hears of gilding the lily but that day it was the hoe. All summer there were still traces of gold clinging to the blades as my husband hilled up the corn.

This year I was gilding angels. I set each one on the kitchen stool and outdoors, since spray paint isn't pleasant to breathe in. In spite of the newspaper covering our red kitchen stool is now touched with gold. But no matter, blue angels, gold angels, silver angels sit in rows in the linen closet where towels are pushed aside. After all, pillow slips, sheets, napkins, and such—what are they compared with angels!

I wish I could find something this glamorous to do with old Sunday papers, Christmas catalogues, and wire coat hangers, all of which seem to accumulate faster than we can dispose of them.

At the rug-hooking group that day after we'd all learned about angels another member came in carrying the loveliest wreath covered with great gold flowers made of artichokes. These are her instructions: Two weeks before Christmas boil artichokes one minute. Drain, run wire through the heart—the part that tastes so good—to hang them with later. Set on newspapers in a warm place and leave. As the head wilts stuff crumpled tissue between the petals to flatten them out. In about two weeks they dry this way and you remove the paper. When completely dry and crisp take outdoors and gild. Never spray too solidly because some of the green showing through is attractive. I left the rug-hooking group that day with my head whirling with new Christmas ideas. Each year we have certain conventional decorations but in addition it is always a pleasure to have something new and different.

Instead of a wreath on the front door Bob cut a triangular shape like a Christmas tree out of a piece of plywood. Over one side of this he tacked chicken wire. We trimmed off some of our lower pine branches cutting them into six- to eight-inch lengths. Beginning at the bottom, I wove these upward through the chicken wire, overlapping them. By the time I reached the top there lay a miniature flat Christmas tree of pine. I arranged the three artichokes down the center from the top to the bottom and looped wide red ribbon where the trunk would be.

As Christmas draws nearer children return from school and college and family members from far and near gather. Fires glow on festive hearths. Neighbors' house lights prick a welcome through the dark. Everywhere a holiday mood prevails. Stores are fragrant with evergreens. Boxes of holly branches don't merely suggest Christmas, they are Christmas. Long ropes of greenery twine over bins of carrots, beets, and fresh lettuces. Baskets of shiny, round red lady apples, and candied fruits and citrons for Christmas baking enhance the vegetable counters. Everywhere rainbows of lights blossom on outdoor evergreens. Daybreak Nursery is a pageant. The Christmas trees along the river in Westport twinkle with lights and a number of similar ones march up the Post Road past the Clam Box.

A few years ago I evolved a system of Christmas shopping which I have followed since. On a holiday I love buying things, especially in Europe where such irresistible presents are available. Everyone delights in Christmas gifts from far places, so in summer we effortlessly accumulate and tuck everything away for Christmas. By December the study drawers are bursting with wonderful gifts and there is very little needed when stores are crowded and confusion reigns.

While I wrap the presents I have the fun of reliving the trip too. I remember that sunny afternoon in the little Alpine village when, after returning from a climb up through the flower meadows, I discovered the scarf obviously woven for my sister Connie, another for our daughter-in-law Susan, and those mittens surely are right for Jesse and Jeff. My summer shopping never solves every purchase, naturally, nor the dinner and food situation, so, like everyone else, I get involved with lists and THINGS.

Sooner or later, however, the more meaningful part of Christmas catches up and obliterates the memory of hurried days. Perhaps a shimmering bit of tinsel or the smell of evergreen stirs something within that was waiting and hoping. This year it happened to me on the street in Westport. The sun was setting golden and the light fading when the sound of chimes rang through the air. I stopped and listened to the clear notes of "Oh, Little Town of Bethlehem"—first time I'd heard it for twelve months. People bent on holiday business moved past me coming and going. A few minutes before they had all appeared as tired and rushed as I had felt. Now they looked quite different. They were smiling and bubbling over with holiday excitement. A great warmth flowed from me towards everyone there on that street—and then the feeling seemed to reach out beyond these strangers, to people everywhere.

Activities the latter part of December mount and gather momentum. Things happen fast. Days blur into a lovely confusion of holiday smells, the fragrance of hot mince pie, and wood smoke burning; the laughter of small children, and long yellow pigtails shining in the light from Christmas tree balls. Neighbors drop in bringing cheese from Holland, cookies with green sparkles and shaped like little Christmas trees, sugar-sweet and crisp. And all the while there is the comfortable sound of the family cricket who lives in the kitchen cupboard and goes about his daily cricket business quite undisturbed.

One evening as Bob and I were driving home and neared our mailbox a red fox dashed out from beside the road and crossed over in front of the car. In the headlights his glowing red coat and full bushy tail gleamed. I've had a few black cats cross my path before but never a red fox. Surely this during Christmas week brings special good luck.

It was Christmas Eve, the last package was wrapped, the tree trimmed, the yule log in. Bob and I stood in the open doorway looking out into the snowy evening. Flakes had been drifting down all day, some huge, some small. It wasn't the kind of sifting fine snow that swirls treetop high, blown into every crack and crevice by that ominous wind that begins a blizzard. Nature was in a gentler mood. We were going to have a white Christmas. This we always welcome, especially if it is brought by a friendly snow that decorates the evergreens, cocks rakish elfin hats on the sturdy stumps that border the drive and settles large frosted "birthday cakes" on the circular bird feeders on the terrace.

Today particularly we welcomed the snow because Joan and Jesse and Jeff were coming to spend the holiday with us and the boys like to ski. We thought we'd heard the sound of their car coming up the lane. We were mistaken but we stood in the doorway for a few moments anyway—it was so beautiful, looking out into the silence, into the whiteness, and watching the flakes float down.

In a few minutes we turned back into the house, Bob to his book and I to my hooked rug until they came. The Christmas tree stood at one side of the room. The window next to it caught and reflected the colored balls, and we had two trees, actually four if you saw it from one certain angle. Festoons of lovely many-toned lights sparkled against the fragrant branches.

At the top of our tree was a tinsel star, rather tarnished because it had been on many trees for many years. This star had always shone from the Christmas tree in the house where I was born and grew up. After we were married it had topped our first Christmas tree—the one with three balls, one for each of the three weeks we'd been married.

Whenever I looked at this star past years came into sharp focus, a snatch of this Christmas, a brief moment of that. And now as it caught the firelight, memory stirred. Looking back through the years can be rather like walking down a dark corridor holding a candle. Incidents and places completely forgotten appear out of the blackness and, one by one, are lit as you pass. There was the Christmas we had a brand new one-month-old daughter tucked in her crib. We were trimming a table-sized tree in our first apartment, and Bob attached this star to the top—really too large for that small tree.

Another Christmas several years later—that same crib had a different baby in it, our third. Tim lay, one tiny finger curled over a blue blanket while two-year-old Bob and five-year-old Joan were hanging stockings, eyes alert, as they listened for the sound of reindeer on the roof.

The fragrance of mince pie and evergreens and a great turkey being stuffed filled the air. I was surreptitiously pressing the Santa Claus outfit Bob would don, and combing out the beard he would wear next morning when he came in with a pack full of presents.

This star at the top of our tree tonight had watched these children grow, seen Joan off to college, and Bob off to Korea, and welcomed him back, had seen Tim off to Alaska and greeted him upon his return.

It had shone down on the first Christmas Bob and I had spent alone together when the children were grown, married and far away.

And now that sound was surely the car bringing our grandsons. Yes, we heard the boys' voices. Out of the snowy night they came, our daughter, Jesse and Jeff, their arms filled with bundles of all shapes and sizes, their faces shining, their eyes glowing.

Our tinsel star again looked down on the Christmas scene. In the midst of holly and tissue paper, candlelight and laughter we gathered around the tree and sang together "Hark The Herald Angels Sing," "Silent Night," and other favorites while Joan accompanied us on the Irish harp.

Later Jeff and Bob were arranging gifts beneath the tree.

"Grandpa, have you thought lately about buying an alligator?" Jeff asked sliding a green package over next to a red one under a branch.

"Well, no, Jeff, I haven't given it much thought recently, have you?"

"Yes, I have, quite a lot, but then I have also been thinking about getting a snake, a nice indigo snake. They feel so smooth. But I think more about an alligator. Alligators are cool."

Before we went to bed we heard the plow in our driveway. Even on Christmas Eve Joe Gjuresko, who plows for the town, hadn't forgotten us. What a good sound is that familiar rumble, as his tractor pushes aside the snow in the drive.

In the quiet house that night, after Bob and I had settled our family, we stood looking at the Christmas tree. The lights glowed and the tinsel star shone down. The snow had stopped and we glanced out the window at stars that pricked through the blackness.

I began wondering about the animals, the shrew, the fox and the deer and all the others outside there going their quiet ways this Christmas Eve, following their own particular stars.

What did Christmas mean to all these creatures of the wilderness, and the others—rabbits, woodchucks, and our birds that visit the feeders and even the cricket in the kitchen? Their world must feel the Christmas season, if differently. Surely some instinct tells them that the shortest day has come and gone this week, that little by little the sun will rise higher in the heavens now. Each day will be longer though imperceptibly at first.

Before turning out the lights we again admired the tree. It did look lovely—with a touch of magic, a touch of mystery in all the gay and colorful packages. And then the family star at the top sparkled there in our living room, a symbol of the new star that guided the three Wise Men on their journey to the wondrous Babe in the manger. Long centuries ago these travellers from afar, bringing myrrh and incense, and bearing precious gifts, had honored the beginning of a new life—a new life that was to change the world. But this the loveliest of all the Bible stories speaks for today as well. I find what it has to tell in my Christmas wish for all of us, and for people everywhere. May we watch for the new stars that appear in our heavens this year and always, and be ready to recognize them, listen to their messages of new beginnings, and follow where they lead.

Index of Recipes and Projects